"Children, darkness reigns over the whole world. People are attracted by many things and they forget about the more important. Light won't reign in the world until people accept Jesus, until they live His words, which is the Word of the Gospel."

"Dear children, this is the reason for my presence among you for such a long time: to lead you on the path of Jesus. I want to save you and, through you, to save the whole world. Many people now live without faith; some don't even want to hear about Jesus, but they still want peace and satisfaction! Children, here is the reason why I need your prayer: prayer is the only way to save the human race."

The Blessed Virgin Mary to Visionaries at Medjugorje, Bosnia- Herzegovina, July 30, 1987.

Visionary Mirjana Soldo and me displaying this book,
The Ten Secrets of the Blessed Virgin Mary,
after my interview at her home in Medjugorje.

Mirjana told me, "It is good that you wrote the book not to scare people. This is important because a mother never scares her children or gives them reason to be afraid. She gives them hope and love."

"Blessed Mary of Medjugorje does not come to cause fear of the future, but for love and peace in the future with her."

"I will pray that the book gives people hope."

Compliments for
The Ten Secrets of the Blessed Virgin Mary

"Once again Dan Lynch has given us a simple, clear presentation, this time on the much discussed and controverted apparitions of Our Lady at Medjugorje. His argumentation in favor of authenticity deserves a serious hearing. For the goals of Our Lady at Medjugorje touch not only local issues, but have worldwide implications and should be pondered in relation to previous apparitions of Mary, for instance, at Fatima, at Amsterdam (Our Lady of all Nations) and elsewhere."

Peter M. Fehlner, F. I.
Rector of the Shrine of Our Lady of Guadalupe

"I praise Dan Lynch for his work at articulating an understanding of the ten secrets of Medjugorje. I also appreciate his use of favorable comments from persons of authority in the Church in assisting people to 'Not Be Afraid.' The Church's teaching regarding unapproved apparitions is that, 'if they are not condemned one is free to follow them'."

Fr. Charles Becker
Leader of pilgrimages to Medjugorje

"In the days of Fatima no one would have believed what has come of the world today. Our Lady's message in 1917 and 93 years later in Medjugorje has not changed. The message of Our Lady is the eternal message of the Gospels – prayer, fasting, conversion, penance, confession, Eucharist. Dan Lynch reminds us of the many apparitions of Our Lady and her heartfelt warning to 'turn away from sin and be faithful to the Gospel.' Only in embracing Our Lady's call will the world be saved from the road of self destruction. In his book, Dan gives a concise presentation of Our Lady's messages and how we can practically respond in today's world. I pray that all who come in contact with this little book, will take seriously the warning of our heavenly mother, embrace her messages and find true peace within their souls."

Father Jay Finelli
The iPadre Catholic Podcast & Videocast

"Dan Lynch has done a masterful job conveying the messages of the Queen of Peace in a simple and readable style for people of all ages."

"Medjugorje is the extension of the messages of Fatima, and what Dan has written are the keys to peace of mind and soul, and will provide people answers in the midst of any storm."

Ted Flynn, Author

Compliments for
Dan Lynch Productions

Saints of the States

"Too few of the faithful in our great country are aware of the lives and sacrifices of the American Saints. Thank you for your latest book, *Saints of the States*."

> Most Reverend Robert J. Baker
> Bishop of the Diocese of Birmingham
> Co-author, *Cacique, A Novel of Florida's Heroic Mission History*

Our Lady of Guadalupe, Hope for the World

"This book will instruct, encourage and inspire a wide variety of people in the Church and outside the Church. You may be a pro-life activist looking for signs of progress. You may be a priest seeking new ways to call your people to deeper faith. You may be a son or daughter of the Virgin Mary eager to find new ways to honor her. You may be someone considering abortion or wounded by it, and looking for hope. You may be away from the Church looking for a way back, or someone without any background in Catholicism but interested in finding out more. Whoever you are, give this book some of your time, and it will repay you abundantly."

> Fr. Frank Pavone, National Director Priests for Life

Our Lady of Guadalupe, Mother of Hope Video

"Stirring, gripping, comprehensive with moving testimonies!"

> Reviews by producers, Ted Flynn, Dr. Tom Petrisko,
> Drew Mariani and Ignatius Press

Compliments for
Dan Lynch Productions

Our Lady of America, Our Hope for the States

"Are there sound grounds for hope about the immediate future of the USA? Without doubt the messages of Our Lady of America to Sr. Mary Ephrem certainly do offer such grounds. This simple, yet detailed sketch of the historical background and of the context of these messages makes perfectly clear why this is so and why Our Lady has chosen the States for a particular role in the salvation of souls, and what will be the consequences of not corresponding with her requests. Dan Lynch once again has succeeded in making crystal clear why the Immaculate Virgin is not simply a pious extra for us, but someone who must be at the very heart of our lives, socially as well as personally."

Fr. Peter M. Fehlner, F.I.
Mariologist and Rector of the Shrine of Our Lady of Guadalupe

Teresita's Choices

"This book is a drama with many surprising twists and turns. While feminists claim that a key aspect of feminism is to 'listen to the voices of women', ironically, those who support abortions fail to listen to the voices of those women who testify to the pain and devastation that it brings. Teresita is one of those voices."

Fr. Frank Pavone, National Director Priests for Life

"This book highlights the devastation of abortion, yet gives hope that Our Lord can heal even the most devastating wounds. No doubt an inspiring book of hope. Thank you for this encouraging book."

Judie Brown, American Life League

The Call to Total Consecration

"I used Dan Lynch's book as a resource for my talk on the Total Consecration. Of the many books that I have received, this is one of the very few that I actually read and enjoyed!"

Scott Hahn, Author and Professor of Theology
and Scripture at Franciscan University of Steubenville

THE TEN SECRETS
OF THE
BLESSED VIRGIN MARY

How to Prepare for Their Warnings

Dan Lynch

Copyright © 2011 Dan Lynch

All rights reserved. This book may not be published or in any way reproduced in whole or in part, stored in a retrieval system, or transmitted, in any form or by any means, electronic, mechanical, photocopying, recording, or otherwise, without written permission. Please do not copy without permission.

Published by:
John Paul Press
144 Sheldon Road
St. Albans, VT 05478
www.JKMI.com

ISBN: 978-0-615-29709-5

Printed in the United States of America

Contents

Contents ix
Foreword by Father Svetozar Kraljevic O.F.M. xiii
Preface xv
Sources xvii
Introduction 1
   Miracle of the Sun at Medjugorje 1
   Medjugorje and Blessed Pope John Paul II 3
   Good Fruits of Medjugorje 4
   Introduction to Chastisements 6
   Champion, U.S.A. 8
   Fatima, Portugal 9
   The Third Secret of Fatima 10
   Akita, Japan 14
   Kibeho, Rwanda 14
   Respond Now! 17
1. The Ten Secrets and a Sign 19
   The Beginning of the Apparitions 19
   The Ten Secrets 20
   The Sign 24
   Chastisement Secrets 26
   Be Not Afraid 27
   The State of the World 29
2: How to Prepare for the Secrets 35
   Peace 35
   Conversion 39
   Faith 41
   Prayer and Fasting 45
   Total Consecration to Jesus through Mary 48

3: The Role of the Blessed Virgin Mary in God's Plan of Salvation......51
- The Fallen Angels......52
- The Fall of Man......53
- Mary's Prefigurement in the Old Testament......55
- The Immaculate Conception......55
- The Annunciation......57
- The Visitation and Nativity......58
- The Presentation and the Finding of Jesus in the Temple...58
- The Crucifixion......59
- Pentecost......60
- The Assumption and Coronation......61
- Co-Redemptrix......62
- Mediatrix of All Graces......63
- The Virtues of Mary......65
- The Divine Mary......67

4: Warnings, Chastisements and the New Era of Peace......69
- Warnings and Chastisements......69
- Chastisements of the Innocent......71
- Chastisements and God's Love......72
- Mary, Prophetess of Chastisements......72
- Protection from Chastisements......74
- Hope for the World......76
- The Triumph of the Immaculate Heart of Mary......77
- The New Era of Peace......79

5: How to Respond to Mary's Requests......81
- How to Make a Good Confession......81
- How to Celebrate the Eucharist......84
- How to Read the Bible......88
- How to Pray......89
- How to Pray the Rosary......92
- The Rosary Method......94
- The Rosary Prayers......95
- Joyful Mysteries of the Rosary......98
- Luminous Mysteries of the Rosary......100
- Sorrowful Mysteries of the Rosary......102
- Glorious Mysteries of the Rosary......104

    How to Fast 106
    How to Make the Total Consecration 107
    How to Use Sacramentals 110

6: Interviews 113
    Interview with Visionary Mirjana Soldo by
    Father Tomislav Vlasic 113
    Interview with Visionary Mirjana Soldo by Dan Lynch . . 124

7: The Status of the Church's Ruling on Medjugorje 129

Appendices 133
    A. The Prayers for Protection of the Jesus, King of
    All Nations, Devotion and Angel Protection Prayers 133
    B. The *I Can Do This!* Checklist for the Laity 137

Bibliography 139

Order Form 141

Foreword by Father Svetozar Kraljevic O.F.M.

Father Svetozar made the following remarks upon my presentation of this book to him at his residence in Medjugorje:

"Dan, we met many years ago and from the beginning in Medjugorje, we have this most amazing phenomenon of people coming and investing their lives for the work of Our Lady. And this phenomenon continues on.

So, when I see this book, I see really a life — life that is broken into the pieces of these sentences for all of us to receive this wonderful inspirational witness and the moving story of another human being who is willing to give so much for the work of the Lord and for the life of the Church.

So I see this book as the blood flowing in the body of the Church, as really the real life of the Church. I see it as the moment of outpouring of the Holy Spirit that will touch each reader. This is what we need now in this aggression of this secular thinking, in this aggression of godless logic.

It is wonderful to have a testimony, to have a book, to have a word spoken to us, to our humanity, to our time, to our children, in the name of God. So Dan, I really thank you for being such a powerful witness of Our Lady."

Preface

The Blessed Virgin Mary, mother of Jesus Christ, true God and true man, was assumed body and soul into heaven after her life on earth in the first century. Since then, she has returned to earth many times in apparitions throughout the world. She comes to offer hope and consolation and, especially since the twentieth century, she requests conversion and prayer and warns of punishments or chastisements if her requests are not followed.

On June 16, 1983, she came from heaven and appeared to six children visionaries in Medjugorje, (pronounced Medge-you-gorey-ay) Bosnia-Herzegovina. She said, *"I have come to tell the world that God exists. He is the fullness of life, and to enjoy this fullness and peace,* **you must return to God**.*"* (Quotes from Mary and Jesus are in italics, bold is for emphasis.)

Do you believe this? Will you return to God and accept His will for your life? This was the question that passenger Fred Beretta had to answer as US Airways flight 1549 approached the Hudson River in New York on January 15, 2009.

Seconds before the plane hit the river, God asked Fred, **"Where will you turn to now? Will you reconcile and trust? You must choose."** As the plane hurtled towards the water and his expected death, the flight attendants kept repeating, "Brace for impact, brace for impact!" A surge of adrenaline coursed through Fred's body and the world seemed to come to a sudden halt. The silent voice came again, *"Will you accept my will for your life?"*

Fred knew he needed to reconcile to the fact that he was not in control. He had two choices, he later wrote, "Either in pride and anger turn away from God or in humility turn fully to Him and accept His will, however inscrutable it was and regardless of the consequences. The river was coming for me and I had to decide."

Fred chose to accept God's will and he and all of the other passengers survived the airplane's crash landing on the Hudson River. This was called the "Miracle on the Hudson." (Beretta, Frederick, *Flight of Faith*. Charlotte, North Carolina: St. Benedict Press, 2009, pp. 36-37).

The river of death and judgment is also coming for each of us and each of us is called to answer "yes" to the question that God put to Fred, *"Will you accept my will for your life?"* This book will tell you how to do so.

The Blessed Virgin Mary's revelations at Medjugorje began in 1981. She gave ten secrets to several of the visionaries which contain warnings and prophesy chastisements for all mankind. The warnings will be events on earth that will be given for those who live as if God does not exist. After the first two secrets or warnings, Mary will leave a visible supernatural sign on the mountain where she first appeared. By that time it will be too late to be converted, so she implored us, "*Hurry to be converted. I need your prayers and your penance.*" (April 25, 1983).

Mirjana (pronounced Mere-yah-nah) Soldo, one of the Medjugorje visionaries, said that we should prepare ourselves for what will happen when the ten secrets revealed by Mary occur. She said, "Yes, prepare! **The Madonna said people should prepare themselves spiritually, be ready, and not panic; be reconciled in their souls. They should be ready for the worst, to die tomorrow. They should accept God now so that they will not be afraid.** They should accept God, and everything else. No one accepts death easily, but they can be at peace in their souls if they are believers. If they are committed to God, He will accept them."

Mary did not reveal the ten secrets to frighten us, but to give us a chance to prepare for them and to protect ourselves from them. The late Father Slavko Barbaric, former Medjugorje parish priest, said, **"The Madonna did not come to announce catastrophes, but more to help us avoid them.** We all know that a nuclear war is possible, even without apparitions. If the house burns, it doesn't burn because the mother cries 'fire.' On the contrary, the mother comes to save the house, which is burning. In that there is hope."

At Fatima, on May 11, 2010, Pope Emeritus Benedict XVI said, "The Church must relearn conversion, prayer, penance. . . . The Virgin Mary came from heaven to remind us of the Gospel truths that constitute for humanity — so lacking in love and without any hope for salvation — the source of hope."

This book explains the revelations about the secrets, warnings and chastisements prophesied by the Blessed Virgin Mary (sometimes referred to as "Our Lady") at Medjugorje since 1981 and how to prepare for them as she requested.

Sources

The basic sources for the information about the ten secrets in this book are exclusive interviews of the visionary Mirjana Soldo with the following people in chronological order: Father Tomislave Vlasic, Father Svetozar Kraljevic, Janice Connell, Padre Livio Fanzaga, and Dan Lynch, the author. The interviews by Father Vlasic and me are contained in Chapter 6.

Mirjana is the only visionary used as a source for the ten secrets because she is the most educated and the most mature of them. She told Father Vlasic that Mary told her that she was "more mature than the others and therefore [she] must help them...."

Moreover, Mirjana has spoken more than any of the other visionaries about the ten secrets. Medjugorje priest, Father Svetozar Kraljevic, O.F.M., wrote that Mirjana "has given the clearest and most descriptive accounts of the apparitions and messages."

Father Tomislav Vlasic O.F.M. moved to Medjugorje in August of 1981, two months after the apparitions began. He was an associate pastor and spiritual advisor to the visionaries until September of 1984, after which he left.

Sadly, Father Vlasic was later reported to the Congregation for the Doctrine of the Faith for various alleged canonical infractions and sins. Father Vlasic did not respond to the reports. Because of that, specific ecclesiastical sanctions and the censure of Interdict were imposed on him in 2008.

In 2009, Pope Emeritus Benedict XVI accepted the request of Father Vlasic and granted him the favor of reduction to the lay state, and of dismissal from the Franciscan Order. The Holy Father also granted him "the remission of the censure incurred as well as the favor of dispensation from religious vows and from all the responsibilities connected with sacred ordination, including celibacy."

The following precepts were imposed on the now *Mr.* Tomislav Vlasic: absolute prohibition from exercising any form of apostolate; from releasing declarations on religious matters, especially regarding the "phenomenon of Medjugorje"; and from prohibition from residing in houses of the Order of Friars Minor.

The Decree against Mr. Vlasic did not find him guilty of the prior alleged reports, to which he did not respond. The Decree is simply a merciful response to his request to be laicized. The Decree does not sanction or discipline the Medjugorje visionaries, apparitions or the parish. It only applies to Mr. Vlasic.

Notwithstanding this Decree, the writings and interviews of Father Vlasic before he left Medjugorje in 1984 are still authoritative. During the time he was in Medjugorje, he interviewed several visionaries on various occasions and in 1983 he wrote a letter concerning the apparitions and messages to Blessed Pope John Paul II.

Father Svetozar Kraljevic O.F.M., who served in Medjugorje with Father Vlasic, printed the entire transcript of Father Vlasic's interview in his book, one of the first books about Medjugorje, *The Apparitions of Our Lady at Medjugorje*. Father Svetozar personally told me that this interview by Father Vlasic "is believable."

Father Svetozar Kraljevic O.F.M. studied philosophy and theology in Sarajevo and Washington DC.

Father Svetozar arrived in America in 1975, was ordained a priest in 1977 in Chicago, and did pastoral work in Chicago and New York. He returned to Medjugorje in 1983, two years after the apparitions began. He wrote books and articles and spoke at many conferences about them. He now lives in Medjugorje where he gives talks to the many pilgrims and administers the apostolate of Mothers Village, a community for orphans, abused women and addicts.

Janice Connell founded the Pittsburgh Marian Center of Peace with her husband, Ed. She is the author of the following books: *The Visions of the Children: the Apparitions of the Blessed Mother at Medjugorje; Queen of the Cosmos* and *Meetings with Mary*.

Padre Livio Fanzaga is the director of Radio Maria, an apostolate located in Medjugorje. He is the author of several books in Italian, including, *La Madonna Prepara per il Mondo un futuro di Pace*. [*The Madonna Prepares the World for a Future of Peace*], which contains an interview with Mirjana.

Introduction

When the Blessed Virgin Mary came to earth in the past, she left supernatural signs in order to help people to believe in her apparitions and messages.

On December 12, 1531 in Mexico, God left her image on the cloak of St. Juan Diego which has defied scientific explanation and still exists today for all to see in the Basilica of Our Lady of Guadalupe in Mexico City.

On October 13, 1917 at Fatima, Portugal, God manifested the so-called "Miracle of the Sun." Contrary to the laws of nature, the sun appeared as an opaque, spinning disc in the sky like a wheel of fire with all the colors of the rainbow. Similarly, the Miracle of the Sun has occurred many times at Medjugorje.

Miracle of the Sun at Medjugorje

On August 2, 2009, a congregation of 50,000 pilgrims gathered on Apparition Hill in Medjugorje to witness an apparition of the Blessed Virgin Mary to visionary Mirjana Soldo. By 5:00 a.m., the whole inner section surrounding the Blue Cross was filled with pilgrims. There were many youth who were sprawled out in sleeping bags, having spent the night on the mountain in anticipation of Mary's early morning apparition. It was an incredible sight, with a sea of faces everywhere you looked, according to an eyewitness.

The apparition of Mary began at 8:45 a.m. and lasted approximately four minutes. Shortly after the apparition began, cries of surprise, shock, deep emotion and awe were heard rippling through the crowd from different directions, growing in magnitude, while Mirjana was enraptured in her vision of Mary.

The pilgrims began to point at the sun. Many witnessed the sun "dancing" or "spinning"; others saw a Cross illuminated in the sun; still others saw different colors spinning off the sun in many directions. Tears were streaming down many faces; others were watching in wonder; others in joy.

After the apparition, Mirjana said that she saw the sun behind the Blessed Virgin Mary during the entire apparition, which was a sign of

Mirjana Soldo in ecstasy seeing the Blessed Virgin Mary with a posture that shows her openness to her love.

the love of Jesus shining down upon the tens of thousands of pilgrims gathered there.

Mary told Mirjana, "*Dear children, I am coming, with my motherly love, to point out the way by which you are to set out, in order that you may be all the more like my Son; and by that, closer to and more pleasing to God. Do not refuse my love.* **Do not renounce salvation and eternal life for the sake of transience and frivolity of this life. I am coming to lead you and, as a mother, to caution you. Come with me.**"

Regarding the Miracle of the Sun, a pilgrim said, "I have been here to Medjugorje about forty times but I have never seen such a miracle as I saw at Mirjana's apparition. After the apparition, I looked up at the sun and it became like a ball and was spinning very fast. People could look at the sun without sun glasses or protection over their eyes. There were many circular waves around the sun like ripples from a stone thrown into the water, which were changing colors from blue to gray."

"At the end of this miracle," the pilgrim continued, "I looked at the Cross on Cross Mountain and around it there were like clouds rising up."

"They were green and yellow and they looked like columns and then some of the people began to cry; many were praying. It was very beautiful. Inside of me was a very strong and powerful feeling of God's love and peace. It was a great experience for my heart."

Pilgrims in awe viewing the Miracle of the Sun.

Medjugorje and Blessed Pope John Paul II

Blessed Pope John Paul II called Medjugorje "the confessional of the world" and said that if he were not Pope that he "would be living in Medjugorje as a priest helping to hear confessions." On April 6, 1995, he made public his desire to go to Medjugorje and wrote to friends in Poland, "We every day return to Medjugorje in prayer." He concluded his daily private Rosary in the Vatican gardens with the prayer, "Our Lady of Medjugorje, pray for me."

He told visiting pilgrims in Rome, "Our Lady of Medjugorje will save America." He wrote to friends in his own hand, "I thank Sophia for everything concerning Medjugorje. I too go there every day as a pilgrim in my prayers. I unite in my prayers with all those who pray there or receive a calling from prayer from there. Today we have understood this call better. I rejoice that our time is not lacking in people of prayer and apostles. Medjugorje is better understood these days. I myself am very much attached to that place."

Mirjana spoke about Blessed Pope John Paul II and Medjugorje. On October 3, 2009, she was asked whether she had ever met with Blessed Pope John Paul II. Mirjana answered, "I am the only one of six visionaries who was lucky enough, had the honor, to encounter Blessed Pope John Paul II. You can imagine how the other five are jealous of me," she said with a smile.

"I was in the Vatican," she continued, "St. Peter's Basilica, with an Italian priest. The Holy Father was walking by and he was blessing us. When he approached me, he blessed me and he just continued to walk. However, this Italian priest loudly said to him, 'Holy Father, this is Mirjana from Medjugorje.'"

"The Pope came back and blessed me again. As he left, I said to the priest, 'He just thinks I need a double blessing.' But then after, he received a note, an invitation to Castel Gandolfo, close to Rome, in order to see the Pope. I couldn't sleep all night because I really loved him and I respected him and I could really feel his love for Our Lady."

"So the next day when he and I met alone, I was just crying. I couldn't say a word because I was so excited. He noticed that I was excited. I think he tried to talk to me in Polish because he thought in the Slavic languages there are things in common. I didn't understand a word!"

"But finally I had enough strength and courage to ask him, 'What are you trying to tell me?' Then we talked. Among other things he said to me, 'I know everything about Medjugorje. I've been following Medjugorje. Ask pilgrims to pray for my intentions, to keep, to take good care of Medjugorje, because **Medjugorje is hope for the entire world. And if I were not Pope, I would have been in Medjugorje a long time ago.**'"

"A priest told me that from the very beginning," Mirjana continued, "the Pope was very fond of Medjugorje because two months before the apparitions in Medjugorje started, the Pope was praying to Our Lady to come again on earth. He said, 'I cannot do it all alone because Yugoslavia, Czechoslovakia, Poland etc, are all Communist, I cannot do it on my own. I need you.' And later he heard that in Yugoslavia, a Communist country, in a little village, Our Lady appeared. Then he said, 'That is a response to my prayers.'"

Mirjana concluded, "On the Mount of Apparitions, I saw a pair of shoes of the Pope in front of me. After the apparition, the gentleman who brought these shoes (he didn't introduce himself) said, 'It was the Pope's desire for a long time to come to Medjugorje. So I said to him, 'If you do not go, I will take your shoes.' And that is how I brought his shoes, so they may be present during the apparition.'" And that is how the Pope's desire to come to Medjugorje was satisfied.

Good Fruits of Medjugorje

The Medjugorje revelations are not yet officially approved or disapproved by the Catholic Church, which awaits future developments such as the fulfillment of the prophesied secrets, warnings and chastisements. Currently, the Vatican has formed a commission to study the revelations.

Our response to Mary's requests at Medjugorje is not dependent on the commission's approval. These requests do not differ from other similar requests from God or Mary that are Church approved, such as at Fatima, Portugal, in 1917; Akita, Japan, in 1973; and at Kibeho, Rwanda, in 1981, which was approved, *after* the prophesied chastisement of a savage genocide occurred there.

Moreover, there are good fruits from Medjugorje that give us reason to believe in the prophecies of Mary. Austrian Cardinal Christopher Schönborn made a pilgrimage to Medjugorje from December 28, 2009 to January 2, 2010. Cardinal Schönborn is a former student and personal friend of Pope Emeritus Benedict XVI. He is the President of the Austrian Bishops' Conference and a member of the Congregation for the Doctrine of the Faith. He is well known for his work as editorial secretary of the *Catechism of the Catholic Church*, his contributions to the Pontifical Theological Commission and his numerous scholarly publications.

During the Cardinal's pilgrimage, he celebrated New Year's Eve Midnight Mass in St. James Church, met with several Franciscan priests and heard confessions. He also visited the hillside where the Blessed Virgin Mary appears.

While the Cardinal was in Medjugorje he said, "[Medjugorje] is about faith in Christ, prayer, the Eucharist, about lived love of neighbor, about the essentials of Christianity and the strengthening of Christian daily life. I always used to say what Jesus has said in the Gospel: 'You will recognize the tree by its fruits.' When I see the fruits of Medjugorje back at home I can only say that the tree is surely good." He then gave examples of these good fruits:

> I will give you a couple of examples: vocation calls for the priesthood. Many of our young priests have received their vocation call here, but not strictly in Medjugorje but because of Medjugorje.
>
> The second thing is conversions. I am impressed that conversions happen in every level of society, from noble families and industrialists down to the common little people. While I was flying from Vienna, via Zagreb to Split I was asked by a security guard where I was going and I told him I was going to Medjugorje. All of a sudden his face started shining and he told me that he had his conversion in Medjugorje as well. A couple of weeks ago on a small railway station a worker told me his story. His wife died of cancer and he was desperate and his friends brought him to Medjugorje. He received a strong and living faith over here.
>
> The third evidence is the healings. A young man who was addicted to drugs told me that he was almost forced by his friends

to come over here. He told me that while the bus was entering Medjugorje, something happened with him. He was healed immediately and all of us know how long that healing lasts.

The fourth evidence is the prayer groups. I've known a Medjugorje Prayer Group from Vienna since before I became a Bishop. I've known them since the 1980s. To us Dominicans it was very meaningful that these people pray for hours and their church is always full. The Dominican churches in Vienna are rarely so full, on Thursday nights the church was always full. They have stayed faithful to the prayer until today. Jesus said that the bad tree doesn't bear any fruits. Which means that if the fruits are good, than the tree is good as well.

These good fruits of Medjugorje should help us to believe Mary's prophesied chastisements in her apparitions there. The status of the Church's ruling on the apparitions and messages of Medjugorje is contained in Chapter 7.

Introduction to Chastisements

God has a perfect will that we should love Him and one another. He also has a permissive will, whereby He permits us to exercise our own free will, which is a gift from Him, to hate Him and one another.

This is a simple explanation of how a God of love can chastise us Himself or allow others to do so and to allow human suffering, hate and violence. However, in His mysterious providence all of these work for the good. (See Romans 8:28). **(If you read the scriptural citations in this book, you will enhance your understanding.)**

The Book of Judith tells us how the God of love allowed His Chosen People, the Jews, to suffer at the hands of the Assyrians and their general Holofernes. He cut off their water supply and laid siege against them for 34 days.

The Jews were prostrate from thirst and exhaustion and saw this as God's vengeance for their sins and the sins of their forefathers. But Judith, a holy widow, did not see this as God's vengeance against them, but as a warning for them to turn to Him.

Judith said, "Not for vengeance did the Lord put [their forefathers] in the crucible to try their hearts, nor has He done so with us. **It is by way of admonition that He chastises those who are close to Him**." (Judith 8:27).

In His providence, God delivered the Jews through the hands of Judith, who cut off the head of Holofernes in his tent with his own sword. This led to the panic and retreat of the Assyrian army whom the Jews pursued and defeated.

A chastisement is an act of God's love to bring us to repentance and peace with Him. It is not vengeance that God exacts, but a punishment sent by God or by others, and allowed by God, such as the Roman's destruction of Jerusalem, in order to help sinners to convert.

God allows chastisements to serve His divine plan of love, to help awaken the consciences of our souls and thereby to turn our hearts and minds to Him, our God and Savior. Through these chastisements we can participate in Christ's redemptive act by sharing in His sufferings.

Chastisements hang over the nations of the world because of the enormity of sin, outright denial and hatred of the one, true God. If we do not convert and return to Him, **He punishes us because He loves us and wants to correct us.**

God will not be ridiculed forever. As St. Paul tells us, "Make no mistake: God is not mocked." (Galatians 6:7). Again and again God has appealed to mankind to turn from their evil and sinful ways. He longs to forgive us and to pour out His great mercy upon us rather than His perfect justice.

As the prophet Micah tells us, "Who is there like you, the God who removes guilt and pardons sin for the remnant of His inheritance; who does not persist in anger forever, but delights rather in clemency, and will again have compassion on us, treading underfoot our guilt? You will cast into the depths of the sea all our sins." (Micah 7:16-19).

In his first encyclical, *Deus Caritas Est (God is Love)*, Pope Emeritus Benedict XVI invites us to recall that "even in their bewilderment and failure to understand the world around them, **Christians continue to believe in the 'goodness and loving kindness of God'.** (Titus 3:4)". (No.38).

Nevertheless, what good and loving father would not correct his children? There are many examples of chastisements in the Bible, such as the Great Flood (see Genesis 6:5) and the destruction of Sodom and Gomorrah (see Genesis 28: 20).

Of course, chastisements are not limited to the Old Testament. As St. Paul tells us in the New Testament, "with flaming power He will inflict punishment on those who do not know God nor heed the good news of Our Lord Jesus." (2 Thessalonians 1:8).

This book teaches us how to prepare for the secrets and chastisements prophesied by the Blessed Virgin Mary at Medjugorje. Prophesied secrets and chastisements from Mary are nothing new. She gave secrets and warned of chastisements before she came to Medjugorje. Mary warned of chastisements at Champion, Fatima, Akita and Kibeho.

Champion, U.S.A.

In the only approved apparition of the Blessed Virgin Mary in the United States of America, Mary made a request and gave a warning if it was not fulfilled. In October of 1859, at Robinsonville (now Champion), Wisconsin, 18 miles northeast of Green Bay, she appeared to Adele Brise, a devout 28-year-old Belgian farm woman.

According to Sister Pauline LaPlant, to whom Adele often told her story, Mary told Adele:

> *I am the Queen of Heaven, who prays for the conversion of sinners, and I wish you to do the same. You received Holy Communion this morning, and that is well. But you must do more. Make a general confession, and offer Communion for the conversion of sinners.* **If they do not convert and do penance, my Son will be obliged to punish them.** . . . *Gather the children in this wild country and teach them what they should know for salvation. Teach them their catechism, how to sign themselves with the sign of the Cross, and how to approach the sacraments; that is what I wish you to do. Go and fear nothing. I will help you.*

Adele obediently began to catechize the children and admonish the sinners of the Bay Settlement. Her father erected a chapel near the spot where Mary appeared.

Apparently the response to Mary's request was not sufficient and on October 8, 1871, almost the 12th anniversary of Mary's apparition, a tremendous fire destroyed 1.2 million acres of Wisconsin and Michigan.

The Great Peshtigo Fire of 1871 is the worst fire in American history. It was described as "a wall of flame, a mile high, five miles wide, traveling 90 to 100 miles an hour, hotter than a crematorium, turning sand into glass." It killed almost 2000 people.

A report stated, "Balls of fire were observed to fall like meteors in different parts of the town [Peshtigo], igniting whatever they came in contact with. By this time the whole population was thoroughly aroused and alarmed, panic-stricken. A brilliant and fearful glare grew suddenly into sight. Men and women snatched their children and ran for the river. Inhaling the burning air, hundreds dropped within sight of the river while many fell within a few feet of the river. Those who reached the river threw water and wet cloths on their heads, and even kept under water as much as they could, and yet were burned to death."

Adele and others sought refuge in the chapel built by her father. There they prayed in terror, begging Mary's intercession for God to save them. The early history reported, "Filled with confidence, they entered the chapel, reverently raised the statue of Mary, and kneeling, bore it in procession around their beloved sanctuary. When wind and fire exposed them to suffocation, they turned in another direction, and continued to hope and pray, saying the Rosary."

Several hours later, their prayers were answered when a rainfall extinguished the fire. There was devastation for miles around but the chapel and its five acres of land, previously consecrated to Mary, were spared. Tongues of fire reached the chapel fence, but the fire did not enter the chapel ground.

On December 8, 2010, Feast of the Immaculate Conception, Bishop David L. Ricken of Green Bay, Wisconsin, issued a formal decree and approved "the events, apparitions and locutions given to Adele Brise in October of 1859." These apparitions are the first in the United States to receive approval of a diocesan bishop.

Fatima, Portugal

In 1917, during World War I, Mary appeared to three young shepherd children at Fatima, Portugal. Pope Emeritus Benedict XVI said, "At a time when the human family was ready to sacrifice all that was most sacred on the altar of the petty and selfish interests of nations, races, ideologies, groups and individuals, our Blessed Mother came from heaven, offering to implant in the hearts of all those who trust in her the love of God burning in her own heart. . . ." (Pope Emeritus Benedict XVI, *Homily at Fatima*, May 13, 2010).

Mary also gave the children secrets and prophesied destruction as a divine chastisement and punishment for sins. She said, "**War is a punishment for sins.**"

On July 13, 1917, Mary showed the children a vision of a large sea of fire, which seemed to be beneath the earth. Sister Lucia, one of the children, later wrote in her memoirs, "Plunged in this fire were the demons and the souls who were like embers, transparent and black or bronze colored, with human forms which floated about in the conflagration, . . . among shrieks and groans of sorrow and despair, which horrified us and caused us to quake with fear."

Mary told the children, "*You have seen hell where poor sinners go. To save them, God wishes to establish in the world devotion to my Immaculate Heart. If what I say to you is done, many souls will be saved and there will be peace in the world.*" She then said that if people did not change and pray, a war worse than World War I would come.

Mary said:

The war is going to end [World War I]; *but if people do not cease offending God, a worse one will break out during the pontificate of Pius XI* [World War II]. *When you see a night illumined by an unknown light,* [which later hovered over Europe], *know that this is the great sign given to you by God that He is about to punish the world for its crimes by means of war, famine and persecutions of the Church and of the Holy Father.*

To prevent this, I shall ask for the consecration of Russia to my Immaculate Heart and a Communion of reparation on the first Saturday of each month. If my appeal is heard, Russia will be converted, and there will be peace. Otherwise, its errors will spread about the world, promoting wars and the persecution of the Church.

The good will suffer martyrdom. The Holy Father will suffer grievously.

In spite of Mary's prophesied warnings, World War II, the rise of Communism and deaths of millions still occurred because of a lack of response to her requests for prayer, especially the daily Rosary.

Sister Lucia, wrote in a letter to Blessed Pope John Paul II on May 12, 1982, **"And let us not say that it is God who is punishing us in this way;** on the contrary it is people themselves who are preparing their own punishment. **In His kindness God warns us and calls us to the right path, while respecting the freedom He has given us; hence people are responsible."**

Mary also said at Fatima, "*Several nations will be annihilated. In the end, my Immaculate Heart will triumph. The Holy Father will consecrate Russia to me, and the earth shall enjoy a period of peace.*"

The revelations of July 13, 1917, came to be known as the two secrets of Fatima, sometimes referred to as two parts of one secret. There was also a third secret shown to them that day, sometimes referred to as the third part of the secret.

The Third Secret of Fatima

Mary revealed another vision to the three children at Fatima on July 13, 1917. This particular vision became known as "The Third Secret of Fatima." A painting of this vision is shown on the following page. The Third Secret vision summarized Mary's message of prayer and penance as the remedies against her prophesied chastisements from God, which would occur if the world did not respond to her requests.

The world did not respond to Mary's requests and her prophecies were

Introduction 11

The Third Secret of Fatima
© St. Andrew's Productions
Used With Permission

fulfilled. However, it is not too late, now, to respond to her requests at Medjugorje, which are a continuation of the Fatima requests, to prepare for the ten secrets that she prophesied there.

The text of the Third Secret of Fatima was released to the world from Vatican City on June 26, 2000 by the Congregation for the Doctrine of the Faith. Sister Lucia, one of the Fatima visionaries, hand wrote the Third Secret vision on paper on January 3, 1944, and wrote:

> At the left of Our Lady and a little above, we saw an angel with a flaming sword in his left hand; flashing, it gave out flames that looked as though they would set the world on fire; but they died out in contact with the splendor that Our Lady radiated towards him from her right hand.
>
> Pointing to the earth with his right hand, the angel cried out in a loud voice: 'Penance, Penance, Penance!'.
>
> And we saw in an immense light that is God: (something similar to how people appear in a mirror when they pass in front of it) a Bishop dressed in white (we had the impression that it was the Holy Father). Other Bishops, priests, men and women Religious going up a steep mountain, at the top of which there was a big Cross of rough-hewn trunks as of a cork-tree with the bark. Before reaching there the Holy Father passed through a big city half in ruins and half trembling with halting step, afflicted with pain and

sorrow, he prayed for the souls of the corpses he met on his way. Having reached the top of the mountain, on his knees at the foot of the big Cross, he was killed by a group of soldiers who fired bullets and arrows at him. In the same way, there died one after another the other Bishops, priests, men and women Religious, and various lay people of different ranks and positions. Beneath the two arms of the Cross there were two angels each with a crystal aspersorium [a sprinkler container] in his hand, in which they gathered up the blood of the Martyrs and with it sprinkled the souls that were making their way to God.

This vision was interpreted by Pope Emeritus Benedict XVI, then Cardinal Joseph Ratzinger, Prefect of the Congregation for the Doctrine of the Faith, on June 26, 2000. He wrote that **the "key word" of the Third Secret of Fatima "is the triple cry, 'Penance, Penance, Penance!'..."**

He also considered the "images" of the Secret and stated, "The angel with the flaming sword on the left of the Mother of God recalls similar images in the Book of Revelation. This represents **the threat of judgment which looms over the world.** Today the prospect that the world might be reduced to ashes by a sea of fire no longer seems pure fantasy: man himself, with his inventions, has forged the flaming sword."

"The vision," he continued, "then shows the power which stands opposed to the force of destruction — the splendor of the Mother of God and, stemming from this in a certain way, the summons to penance. In this way, the importance of human freedom is underlined: **the future is not in fact unchangeably set**, and the image which the children saw is in no way a film preview of a future in which nothing can be changed. Indeed, the whole point of the vision is to bring freedom onto the scene and to steer freedom in a positive direction.... Its meaning is to mobilize the forces of change in the right direction. Therefore we must totally discount fatalistic explanations of the 'secret,' such as, for example, the claim that the would-be assassin [of Blessed Pope John Paul II] of May 13 1981, was merely an instrument of the divine plan guided by Providence.... Rather, **the vision speaks of dangers and how we might be saved from them.**"

Cardinal Ratzinger explained that "the place of the action is described in three symbols: a steep mountain, a great city reduced to ruins and finally a large rough-hewn Cross. The mountain and city symbolize the arena of human history: history as an arduous ascent to the summit, history as the arena of human creativity and social harmony, but at the same time a place of destruction, where man actually destroys the fruits of his own work.... On the mountain stands the Cross — the goal and guide of history. The

Cross transforms destruction into salvation; it stands as a sign of history's misery but also as a promise for history."

"At this point," the Cardinal continued, "human persons appear: the Bishop dressed in white [apparently the Pope] . . . other Bishops, priests, men and women Religious, and men and women of different ranks and social positions. The Pope seems to precede the others, trembling and suffering because of all the horrors around him. Not only do the houses of the city lie half in ruins, but he makes his way among the corpses of the dead. The Church's path is thus described as a 'Via Crucis,' [Way of the Cross] as a journey through a time of violence, destruction and persecution. The history of an entire century can be seen represented in this image. Just as the places of the earth are synthetically described in the two images of the mountain and the city, and are directed towards the Cross, so too time is presented in a compressed way."

"**In the vision we can recognize the last century as a century of martyrs, a century of suffering and persecution for the Church, a century of World Wars and the many local wars which filled the last fifty years and have inflicted unprecedented forms of cruelty.** In the 'mirror' of this vision we see passing before us the witnesses of the faith decade by decade."

The Cardinal also stated that "in the Via Crucis of an entire century, the figure of the Pope has a special role. In his arduous ascent of the mountain we can undoubtedly see a convergence of different Popes. Beginning from Pius X up to the present Pope, [Pope Francis I] they all shared the sufferings of the century and strove to go forward through all the anguish along the path which leads to the Cross. In the vision, the Pope too is killed along with the martyrs. When, after the attempted assassination on 13 May 1981, the Holy Father had the text of the third part of the 'secret' brought to him, was it not inevitable that he should see in it his own fate? He had been very close to death, and he himself explained his survival in the following words: '. . . it was a mother's hand that guided the bullet's path and in his throes the Pope halted at the threshold of death.' (May 13, 1994). That here 'a mother's hand' had deflected the fateful bullet only shows once more that **there is no immutable destiny, that faith and prayer are forces which can influence history and that in the end prayer is more powerful than bullets and faith more powerful than armies.**"

"The conclusion of the secret," continued the Cardinal, "uses images which Lucia may have seen in devotional books and which draw their inspiration from long-standing intuitions of faith. It is a consoling vision, which seeks to open a history of blood and tears to the healing power of God. Beneath the arms of the Cross angels gather up the blood of the martyrs, and with it they give life to the souls making their way to God. Here, the blood of Christ and the blood of the martyrs are considered as one: the blood of the martyrs runs down from the arms of the Cross. The martyrs die in communion with the Passion of Christ, and their death becomes one with His."

"**The vision of the third part of the 'secret', so distressing at first, concludes with an image of hope: no suffering is in vain, and it is a suffering Church, a Church of martyrs, which becomes a sign-post for man in his search for God.** . . . From the suffering of the witnesses there comes a purifying and renewing power, because their suffering is the actualization of the suffering of Christ himself and a communication in the here and now of its saving effect." . . .

"What remains was already evident when we began our reflections on the text of the 'secret': **the exhortation to prayer as the path of 'salvation for souls' and, likewise, the summons to penance and conversion.**" This was also the summons of Mary at Akita, Japan.

Akita, Japan

In 1973, the Blessed Virgin Mary appeared to Sister Agnes Sasagawa in Akita, Japan. God left a sign to help us to believe in her messages. A statue of her miraculously wept on 101 occasions over the next six years. In June 1988, Joseph Cardinal Ratzinger (later Pope Emeritus Benedict XVI), Prefect of the Congregation for the Doctrine of the Faith, gave a definitive judgment on the Akita events and messages as reliable and worthy of belief. On October 13, 1973, Mary said:

> *If men do not repent and better themselves, the Father will inflict a terrible punishment on all humanity.* It will be a punishment greater than the deluge, [the Great Flood] such as one will never have seen before. Fire will fall from the sky and will wipe out a great part of humanity, the good as well as the bad, sparing neither priests nor faithful. The survivors will find themselves so desolate that they will envy the dead. The only arms which will remain for you will be the Rosary and the Sign left by my Son. Each day recite the prayers of the Rosary. With the Rosary, pray for the Pope, the Bishops and the priests.

Kibeho, Rwanda

In 1981, only four months after the beginning of her apparitions at Medjugorje, Mary began appearing at Kibeho, Rwanda. She emphasized the call to pray the Rosary and asked for penance and fasting, similar to her requests at Fatima, Akita and, now, Medjugorje.

Mary showed the visionaries images of savage murders, machetes, a "river of blood", people brutally killing each other, decapitated bodies, abandoned corpses with no one to bury them, and the putrefying remains of hundreds of thousands. These visions are now considered a prophecy of the ethnic genocide that later took place in their country.

On August 19, 1982, Mary appeared and, according to Father Gabriel Maindron, author of *Kibeho*, "The visionaries sometimes cried, their teeth chattered, they trembled. They collapsed several times with the full weight of their bodies during the apparitions, which lasted nearly eight hours without interruption. The crowd of about 20,000 present on that day was given an impression of fear — indeed, panic and sadness." Apparently Mary herself was sad.

Immaculée Ilibagiza, Rwandan genocide survivor and author of *Our Lady of Kibeho*, wrote that Mary had the visionary, Alphonsine Mumureke, repeat three times into the microphone an apparent lament for the failure to respond to her requests, "**You opened the door and they refused to come in.** You opened the door and they refused to come in. You opened the door and they refused to come in."

Then Immaculée reported, "Suddenly Alphonsine let out a gut-wrenching scream that cut through the startled crowd like a razor, 'I see a river of blood! What does that mean? No, please! Why did you show me so much blood? Show me a clear stream of water, not this river of blood!' the seer cried out, as the Holy Mother revealed one horrifying vision after another. The young woman was subjected to so many images of destruction, torture, and savage human carnage that she pleaded, 'Stop, stop, please stop! Why are those people killing each other? Why do they chop each other?'"

Alphonsine was next shown "a growing pile of severed human heads, which were still gushing blood. The grotesque sight worsened still as Our Lady expanded Alphonsine's vision until she beheld a panoramic view of a vast valley piled high with the remains of a million rotting, headless corpses, and not a single soul left to bury the dead."

Mary gave a clear warning. She said, "**My children, it does not have to happen if people would listen and come back to God.**" She told them to warn government leaders, who belonged to the Hutu tribe, not to battle with the minority Tutsis.

Unfortunately, the warning was not heeded and, twelve years after the first apparitions, the two tribes entered a horrible civil war. One of the slaughters took place on the very spot where Mary had appeared. Twenty-five thousand people were killed in the place where pilgrims once knelt.

The hands of a statue of Mary were shot off during the war and a bullet was embedded in her heart. Three of the visionaries were slaughtered in the mayhem.

Many of the deceased were chopped up and thrown in a river. As prophesied, machete-wielding soldiers killed almost a million Rwandans in the span of a few short months. This was the highest rate of killing in recorded history.

The Kibeho warnings were not just for Rwanda, but for the whole world. Mary said, *"When I tell you this, I am not addressing myself strictly to you, child, but I am making this appeal to the world which is in revolt against God.* **I am concerned with and turning to the whole world to repent because otherwise the world is on the edge of catastrophe."**

On June 29, 2001, the Church approved the Kibeho apparitions in the "Declaration on the Definitive Judgment on the Apparitions of Kibeho." This declaration, written by Rwandan Bishop Augustine Misago and released by the Vatican, proclaimed, "Yes, the Virgin Mary did appear in Kibeho on Nov. 28, 1981," and then over "the course of the following six months. There are more reasons to believe this than to deny it." This approval came *after* Mary's warnings for Rwanda were fulfilled.

The Catholic Catechism teaches us, "Throughout the ages, there have been so-called 'private' revelations, some of which have been recognized by the authority of the Church. They do not belong, however, to the deposit of faith. It is not their role to improve or complete Christ's definitive Revelation, but to help live more fully by it in a certain period of history. Guided by the Magisterium [Teaching Authority] of the Church, the *sensus fidelium* [the sense of the faithful] knows how to discern and welcome in these revelations whatever constitutes an authentic call of Christ or his saints to the Church." (*Catechism of the Catholic Church*, hereafter *CCC*, 67).

So, to help us to live more fully by Christ's Revelation in this period of history, let us discern and welcome in the revelations from Medjugorje the authentic call of the Blessed Virgin Mary to the Church today. As she told one of the visionaries at Rwanda, **"The world is on the edge of catastrophe. Cleanse your hearts through prayer. The only way is God. If you don't take refuge in God, where will you go to hide when the fire has spread everywhere?"**

The Rwandan people did not listen to Mary's motherly guidance and were unable to escape the tragic consequences of the genocide. When the terrifying scenes shown to the visionaries became reality, and the Church approval came, it was simply too late.

Respond Now!

People did not respond to Mary's requests at Champion, Fatima, and Kibeho and they suffered from the prophesied chastisements.

We don't have to wait for the Church's approval of the messages, secrets, warnings and chastisements of Medjugorje before we respond to Mary's requests. If we do, it may be too late, like it was for Champion, Fatima and Kibeho, and they may happen before any approval. We don't even have to believe that Mary appeared or gave any messages at Medjugorje, but we still should respond to her requests. All of her requests listed and explained in this book are consistent with the teachings of the Catholic Church.

Immaculee Ilibagiza, said, "I only share messages not yet approved because, like the title of my fourth book, *If Only We Had Listened,* to Our Lady and Our Lord who warned us to what was going to happen to Rwanda and what to do to avoid it, long before the Church could approve those apparitions, the genocide would not have happened, so it is up to you to discern."

When Pope Emeritus Benedict XVI visited Fatima on May 11, 2010, he said, "The Lord told us that the Church would constantly be suffering, in different ways, until the end of the world. . . . **We need to relearn precisely this essential: conversion, prayer, penance and the theological virtues. This is our response**, we are realists in expecting that evil always attacks, attacks from within and without, yet that the forces of good are also ever present and that, **in the end, the Lord is more powerful than evil and Our Lady is for us the visible, motherly guarantee of God's goodness, which is always the last word in history.**"

During the Mass at Fatima on May 13, in the presence of half a million people, the Pope reaffirmed that "the demanding but consoling message the Virgin left us at Fatima is full of hope. **It is a message that focuses on prayer, penance and conversion, a message projected beyond the threats, dangers and horrors of history, inviting humankind to have faith in the action of God, to cultivate great hope, and to experience the grace of the Lord in order to love Him, the source of love and peace.**". . .

"In Fatima the Blessed Virgin Mary invites us to walk with hope," the Pope continued, "letting ourselves be guided by the 'wisdom from on high' which was manifested in Jesus, the wisdom of love, to bring the light and joy of Christ into the world."

Let us not be caught unprepared. **The time to convert, pray (especially the Rosary), fast and receive the sacraments of Penance and Eucharist is NOW!** Let it not be for us as it was in the days of Noah. Jesus said, "For as it was in the days of Noah, so it will be at the coming of the Son of Man. In those days before the flood, they were eating and drinking, marrying and giving in marriage, up to the day that Noah entered the ark. They did not know until the flood came and carried them all away." (Matthew 24:37-39.).

Let us pray, "Blessed be God who lives forever, whose kingdom is eternal. For He both punishes and then has mercy." (Tobit 13:1-2).

1. The Ten Secrets and a Sign

The Blessed Virgin Mary came from heaven to Medjugorje and revealed ten warnings and secrets. She prophesied that she would leave a permanent supernatural sign on the hill where she first appeared. These will all come to light, for as the Gospel says, "Nothing is secret except to come to light." (Mark 4:22).

The Beginning of the Apparitions

Medjugorje (Croatian for "between the hills") is a remote village located in Bosnia-Herzegovina, surrounded by rocky hills and centered on St. James Church. Approximately thirty million pilgrims of all faiths, races and nationalities have traveled there because of apparitions of the Blessed Virgin Mary. They began on June 24, 1981, the feast of St. John the Baptist, the first herald of Jesus. Now she comes as His modern herald. Like John the Baptist she goes "before the Lord to prepare His ways, to give His people knowledge of salvation through the forgiveness of their sins." (Luke 1:76-77).

The apparitions have continued since 1981. Six visionaries experience the apparitions with their senses and not their imaginations. They see and hear the Blessed Virgin Mary who appears to them as a young lady of about twenty with a beauty that is beyond human description.

Mary identified herself as the Queen of Peace. She said that she came to Medjugorje "*because there are many true believers here.*" (June 26, 1981). She asked, "*that those who do not see believe as those who see.*" (June 28, 1981).

Author Janice Connell reported that visionary Mirjana Soldo described Mary's appearance as, "Dressed in a gray dress, a white veil, [with] that beautiful face [and] those incredibly beautiful eyes of love. Her whole demeanor is filled with God's love."

She told the visionaries that **God sent her to the world to help us to convert our hearts and lives back to her Son, Jesus, true God and true man.** In her motherly love for us, she promised to leave a visible sign on the hill where she first appeared so that the whole world would believe.

Father Tomislav Vlasic O.F.M. wrote Blessed Pope John Paul II a letter dated December 2, 1983, based upon his interviews with some of the visionaries. He wrote, "All of the youngsters basically agree that:

We see the Blessed Virgin just as we see anyone else. We pray with her, we speak to her, and we can touch her.

The Blessed Virgin says that world peace is at a critical stage. She repeatedly calls for reconciliation and conversion.

She has promised to leave a visible sign for all humanity at the site of the apparitions of Medjugorje.

The period preceding this visible sign is a time of grace for conversion and deepening the faith."

Mary told the visionaries:

> *Children, darkness reigns over the whole world. People are attracted by many things and they forget about the more important. Light won't reign in the world until people accept Jesus, until they live His words, which is the Word of the Gospel.*
> **Dear children, this is the reason for my presence among you for such a long time: to lead you on the path of Jesus. I want to save you and, through you, to save the whole world.** *Many people now live without faith; some don't even want to hear about Jesus, but they still want peace and satisfaction! Children, here is the reason why I need your prayer:* **prayer is the only way to save the human race.** (July 30, 1987).

Mary showed some of the visionaries hell. She explained why she did this and said, *"Do not be afraid! I have shown you hell so that you may know the state of those who are there."* (November 6, 1981).

The Ten Secrets

Mary gave several of the visionaries ten secrets each. It is not known if they all have the same secrets. As the prophet Amos tells us, "The Lord God does nothing without revealing His secrets to His servants, the prophets." (Amos 3:7).

Visionary Mirjana Soldo, like the prophet Amos, has her ten secrets. She will reveal them and they will come to light in the fullness of the time of God's sovereign love and providence.

Mirjana told the author that she was born on March 18, 1965, in Sarajevo in what was then Yugoslavia in what is now Bosnia-Herzegovina. She attended the University of Sarajevo for three years. However, it was impossible for her to continue her education because she could not receive permission from the Communist government. They knew her as a "visionary" and she said that she was an enemy of the state and that, "God does not exist in Yugoslavia."

Both of her parents were born in Medjugorje and she used to travel there to visit her grandparents when she lived in Sarajevo. The apparitions of Our Lady began there in 1981, while she was on a visit. Later, she married her husband, Marco, and they moved to Medjugorje in 1989. She now has two teenage daughters, Maria and Veronica.

In his letter to Blessed Pope John Paul II, Father Vlasic summarized the substance of his interview with Mirjana about the secrets. He wrote:

> Mirjana said that before the visible sign is given to humanity, there will be three warnings to the world. The warnings will be in the form of events on earth. Mirjana will be a witness to them. Three days before one of the admonitions, Mirjana will notify a priest of her choice. The witness of Mirjana will be a confirmation of the apparitions and a stimulus for the conversion of the world.
>
> The ninth and tenth secrets are serious. They concern chastisement for the sins of the world. Punishment is inevitable, for we cannot expect the whole world to be converted. The punishment can be diminished by prayer and penance, but it cannot be eliminated. Mirjana says that one of the evils that threatened the world, the one contained in the eighth secret has been averted, thanks to prayer and fasting. [Mirjana told the author that this was a mistake and that it was the seventh secret and not the eighth secret that had been averted.] That is why the Blessed Virgin continues to encourage prayer and fasting: *"You have forgotten that through prayer and fasting you can avert war and suspend the laws of nature."*
>
> After the first admonition, the others will follow in a rather short time. Thus, people will have some time for conversion.
>
> That interval will be a period of grace and conversion. After the visible sign appears, those who are still alive will have little time for conversion. For that reason, the Blessed Virgin invites us to urgent conversion and reconciliation.
>
> The invitation to prayer and penance is meant to avert evil and war, but most of all to save souls.
>
> According to Mirjana, the events predicted by the Blessed Virgin are near. By virtue of this experience, Mirjana proclaims to the world: "Hurry, be converted; open your hearts to God."

Mirjana told me, "I never ask Blessed Mary questions. I just listen to what she tells me. She told me, 'Choose a priest to whom you will tell the first *secret*.' She emphasized the singular. She did not tell me to tell him *all* of the secrets. I chose Father Petar Ljubicic. I'll tell him the first secret ten days before it occurs. We will fast and pray together for seven days and then he will announce the secret three days before it occurs. I don't know if each of the secrets will be announced."

Mirjana continued, "On Christmas Day, 1982, I received the last of my ten secrets. Then Blessed Mary gave me all of the ten secrets. I received these ten secrets at the same time on one thing. It was like ... [Mirjana paused and looked up searching for words] what the Queens wrote on 150 years ago — a scroll! Blessed Mary presented it to me and it contained all ten secrets and I could immediately read it. It was in my house in Sarajevo during the war and it was brought from there to here in Medjugorje for safekeeping."

"Others have seen it and can see something, but they see it differently. I showed it to one of my cousins who saw it as a letter asking for help. I also showed it to a friend who saw it as a prayer. Since then, I have not shown it to anyone else because different people see it in different ways, and only I see it as containing the ten secrets."

"Regarding my release of the first secret, I will not *give* the scroll to Father Petar," Mirjana said. "Blessed Mary told me, 'You will *tell* the priest ten days in advance.' [Mirjana emphasized the word 'tell" in contrast to the word "give".] Blessed Mary never told me to give him the scroll. My only role is to tell Father Petar. All of the secrets are for all of the world, none are just for the parish or the Church. My role is not to distribute the secrets to the world."

Father Petar said, "Three days before it happens, I will be able to tell everybody what will happen: where, at what time, hour, and minute, and how long it will be lasting."

Mirjana told Janice Connell, author of several books on Medjugorje, that she knows the date of each of the secrets and that all of them will occur during her lifetime. She said, "The first two secrets will be warnings to the world — events on the earth as warnings to the world that will occur before the visible sign is given to humanity. **These will happen in my lifetime. That is why Mary's call to conversion is so urgent. She is our mother, and she would like all of us to heed the message she is giving us. She wishes this so that later, when the secrets are to be revealed, there will not be any unbelievers."**

Mirjana told Mrs. Connell that we should not be frightened, because we are God's children and if people only realized how much He loves us, and what He has prepared for us they would be filled with such peace! She added that those who use their freedom to choose things that are not of God will suffer the tortures of children of Satan. God gives His children heaven, but Satan brings his children to hell with them.

Mirjana concluded the interview with Mrs. Connell and said, "My witness will be an affirmation to the world of the authenticity of the apparitions at Medjugorje and a stimulus for the conversion of the world. **After the visible sign, those still alive will have little time for conversion.** God is not cruel! God is love, only love. Cruelty and evil come from Satan. But with our free will we choose God or Satan every moment. **Those who freely choose Satan, who disobey God's commandments, will perish.**"

Mother Mary said, *"Dear Children! God gives me this time as a gift to you, so that I may instruct and lead you on the path of salvation. You do not comprehend this grace, but **soon a time will come when you will lament for these messages**."* (August 25, 1997)

On December 24, 1982, in her next-to-last apparition to Mirjana, Mary told her, *"Mirjana, I selected you and told you all that is necessary. I transferred to you many horrors that you must carry worthily. **Think of me and think about how many tears I have shed because of these horrors.** You must always be courageous."* (Connell, Janice. *The Visions of the Children*. New York, New York: St. Martin's Press, 1992, 1997).

In an interview at Medjugorje on October 3, 2009, Mirjana said, "I never think about the secrets. I don't even think about it, because it is dear God who keeps the secrets and His will be done. For example this morning, I spoke to Italians, maybe you saw there were thousands of them! Any and every question they asked started with, 'Why, why, why, why this, why that, waving their hands.'"

"Then I said to them, 'You know why Our Lady did not appear in Italy but in Croatia?' And they said again, 'Why?' I said if she appeared in Italy she would run away after the third day because it would always be, 'Why, why, why?' Whatever she said, we just accepted it the way it is. I never said 'why' because whatever Our Lady says, that is for our good and it is not up to me to ask 'why'."

Mirjana has never revealed any details of any of the secrets to anyone. There are reports in books and Internet articles that Mirjana had an apparition on October 25, 1985, in which she was supposedly shown a vision of the first secret which was played before her as though it were a film. Mary supposedly told Mirjana, "It is the upheaval of a region of the world." It is also reported that on the next day, Mirjana gave an interview to a priest and supposedly said that the first secret would be "necessary in order to shake up the world a little."

Mirjana emphatically told me that she never had such an apparition or made such statements. She emphasized that her last apparition occurred on December 25, 1982, when she received her tenth and last secret. She had no apparitions after that, especially as alleged on October 25, 1985, except on her birthday, March 18, each year until 1987. Since then, she receives apparitions on the second of the month.

When Padre Livio pressed Mirjana about details of the secrets, she told him, "Look, Father, if we want to continue the interview on important things, about Our Lady and her messages, I'll respond willingly. But I won't speak about the secrets because secrets are secrets! We [visionaries] have been asked about them by everyone from priests to the Communists, particularly who questioned Jakov when he was only nine and a half years old, but we have never revealed the secrets. We always avoided this topic."

Mirjana also told me, "We visionaries do not talk to each other about the secrets, so we don't know if we have the same secrets or not."

Of course everyone is curious to know more about the secrets, Mirjana told Padre Livio that even Father Petar is curious. She said that when he came to Medjugorje from Germany, he joked with her and said, "Tell me at least one secret."

Mirjana told Padre Livio, "What is really important is to be ready to meet the Lord at any time. Everything that happens will be the will of the Lord, and we can't change that, we can only change ourselves."

The Sign

After the first two secrets or warnings, the Blessed Virgin Mary will leave a visible, supernatural, indestructible and permanent sign on the hill where she first appeared in Medjugorje. She said, *"Be converted! It will be too late when the sign comes. Beforehand, several warnings will be given to the world. Hurry to be converted. I need your prayers and your penance."* (April 25, 1983).

Father Vlasic reported in his letter to Blessed Pope John Paul II, "After the admonitions, the visible sign will appear on the site of the apparitions in Medjugorje for all the world to see. **The sign will be given as a testimony to the apparitions and in order to call the people back to the faith. The witness of Mirjana will be a confirmation of the apparitions and a stimulus for the conversion of the world.**"

Mirjana told Padre Livio in his interview in 2001, "There will be a sign on the hill of the apparitions. It will be like a gift for all of us because we will see that the Madonna is here for us as our mother. It will be very beautiful and a very visible sign that can't be made with human hands, it will be something from the Lord that will remain. I know the date of the sign."

The sign will be given for the atheists. The faithful already have signs and must themselves become a sign for the atheists. The faithful must not wait for the sign before they convert. This time is a time of grace for us. We can never thank God enough for His grace. This time is for deepening our faith and our conversion. **When the sign comes, it will be too late for many. As a mother, Mary cautions us because she loves us. The secrets exist. Nothing is known of these now, but when they are known, it will be too late to convert.**

Regarding the sign, Mary further said:

> *The sign will come; you must not worry about it. The only thing I would want to tell you is to be converted. Make that known to all my children as quickly as possible. No pain, no suffering is too great for me in order to save you. I will pray to my Son not to punish the world, but I plead with you, be converted.*
>
> **You cannot imagine what the Eternal Father will send to earth. That is why you must be converted. Renounce everything. Do penance.** *Express my thanks to all my children who have prayed and fasted. I carry all this to my Divine Son in order to obtain an alleviation of His justice against the sins of mankind.*
>
> *I thank the people who have prayed and fasted. Persevere and help me to convert the world.* (June 24, 1983).

Mirjana told Fr. Vlasic in his interview on January 10, 1983, "First, some secrets will be revealed — just a few. Then the people will be convinced that Our Lady was here. Then they will understand the sign. When Jakov [another visionary] said that the mayor will be the first one to run to the hill, he meant that generally, people of the highest social class. They will understand the sign as a place or occasion to convert. They will run to the hill and pray, and they will be forgiven. When I asked Our Lady about unbelievers, she said: 'They should be prayed for, and they should pray.' But when I asked again, recently, she said: 'Let them convert while there is time.' She did not say they should be prayed for."

Medjugorje is not the first place where Our Lady promised a sign. The Blessed Virgin Mary also appeared at Fatima, Portugal in 1917. She warned the world then to convert or to experience a worse war (World War II) than World War I, which was then ravaging Europe. Mary said that war is a punishment for sins. As she has promised at Medjugorje, Mary also promised at Fatima to leave a sign to confirm her warnings of chastisements. She promised that there would be a great public miracle for all to see "so that all may believe." She prophesied the exact date and place of this miracle — October 13, 1917 at Fatima.

On that date, approximately 100,000 people witnessed the "Miracle of the Sun." The sun appeared to defy all cosmic laws. It "danced" and spun in the sky and suddenly fell to earth. After a rainfall, the sun broke through the clouds and appeared as an opaque, spinning disc in the sky, "like the most magnificent firewheel that could be imagined, taking on all the colors of the rainbow and sending forth multicolored flashes of light," according to an eyewitness.

The sun then suddenly fell to the earth in a zigzag pattern causing the previously muddy ground and the wet clothes of the witnesses to become completely dried. Eyewitness José Maria de Almeida Garrett, Professor at the Faculty of Sciences of Coimbra, Portugal, said, "One heard a clamor, a cry of anguish breaking from all the people. The sun, whirling wildly, seemed all at once to loosen itself from the firmament and, blood red, advance threateningly upon the earth as if to crush us with its huge and fiery weight. The sensation during those moments was truly terrible."

Many thought that it was the end of the world, but the sun returned to its place in the sky.

The sign and the fulfillment of the secrets as announced at Medjugorje will be a confirmation to the world of the reality of the apparitions of the Blessed Virgin Mary there and an incentive for the conversion of the world. It will help all people to come to believe and know the love of the one, true God. Don't wait, now is the time to turn to God! We must open our hearts and begin to change our lives starting today, starting right now.

Chastisement Secrets

Concerning the chastisement secrets, Mirjana told Father Vlasic in her interview with him on January 10, 1983:

> I can tell you that the eighth secret is worse than the other seven. [Mirjana subsequently corrected this statement and told me that it was the seventh secret that was worse and that was lessened.] I prayed for a long time that it might be less severe. Every day, when Our Lady came, I pestered her, asking that it be mitigated. Then she said that everyone should pray that it might be lessened. So, in Sarajevo, I got many people to join me in this prayer. Later, Our Lady told me that she'd been able to have the secret lessened. But then she told me the ninth secret and it was even worse. Then tenth secret is totally bad and cannot be lessened whatsoever. I cannot say anything about it, because even a word would disclose the secret before it's time to do so.

Mirjana told Padre Livio, "I asked Our Lady if it was possible that at least part of that secret [the seventh] will change. She said that we had to pray. We prayed a lot and she said that she changed a part, but now we cannot change it anymore, because it is the will of the Lord that must be realized."

She told him, "It is not possible to be abolished altogether. Only one part of it was removed. Our Lady told me that it was mitigated, but now that it must be realized. I do not ask anything more about these things because this is the will of the Lord and it should be done."

Regarding the lessening or mitigation of the punishment, Mary told Mirjana on November 11, 1982, "*I have prayed. The punishment has been softened. Repeated prayers and fasting reduce punishments from God, but it is not possible to avoid entirely the chastisement.* **Go on the streets of the city, count those who glorify God and those who offend him. God can no longer endure that.**"

Although Mirjana said that the tenth secret "cannot be lessened *whatsoever,*" Mary said that "it is not possible to avoid *entirely* the chastisement." This should give us hope that the chastisement need not happen *entirely* and that it may still be lessened.

The threatened biblical chastisement of the destruction of the city of Nineveh was entirely avoided because the people repented. (See Jonah chapter 3). The threatened biblical chastisement of the destruction of Sodom and Gomorrah could have been avoided if enough people repented, but they did not and the twin cities were destroyed. (See Genesis chapter 19). So we should repent and respond to Mary's requests in order to avoid or mitigate the threatened chastisements.

Let us take hope in the words of Pope Emeritus Benedict XVI (then Cardinal Joseph Ratzinger) who interpreted the vision of the Third Secret of Fatima. He wrote on June 26, 2000, "The future is not in fact unchangeably set.... The vision speaks of dangers and how we might be saved from them. ... **There is no immutable destiny, that faith and prayer are forces which can influence history and that in the end prayer is more powerful than bullets and faith more powerful than armies..... What remains ... [is] the exhortation to prayer as the path of 'salvation of souls' and, likewise, the summons to penance and conversion.**"

Be Not Afraid

In an interview at Medjugorje on October 3, 2009, Mirjana said, "I would like to recommend that you not talk about chastisements, because Our Lady came in Medjugorje to help us and not to destroy us. She said, '*What I started in Fatima, I will finish in Medjugorje. My heart will triumph.*' If our Heavenly Mother's heart will triumph, what is there to fear?"

In the same interview, Mirjana said, regarding the end of the world, "Well, the one who dies tomorrow, for that person the end of the world will happen tomorrow. That person will encounter God tomorrow. So it is not important to talk about it at all. It is important to talk about ourselves, to think of myself. **What is my soul like? Is it ready to encounter God now, this very moment?**"

Mirjana told Padre Livio in his interview, "The Madonna always says not to talk about the secrets, but to pray. She says, 'Whoever relates to me like a mother, and to God like a father, has no fear.' The Madonna teaches us not to worry about the future and not to waste time speaking about the secrets, but to be ready to meet the Lord at any moment."

She concluded, "I do not understand why you should be afraid. I just want to say to all my brothers and sisters that you need not fear. **The only ones that should be afraid are those who do not give the Lord first place in their hearts. If you have Our Lord and Our Lady in the first place of your heart, of what should you be afraid?** That's why I do not want people to think that you should be afraid. There can be no fear if God and Our Lady are in first place in your heart."

Jesus said, "**Fear is useless, what is needed is trust.**" (Mark 5:36). Visionary Mirjana Soldo has no fear. She is a joyful woman with a devoted husband and two daughters. When asked why there would be secrets, Mirjana said, "I only know it is God's will and all that is to happen. But I do want to say that there is no reason to fear, because the Blessed Mother does not want faith to come from fear. That faith does not last. There is no reason to fear. She said that if we love God, we have peace of joy, — *no matter what transpires.*"

Because we are God's children, we should not fear anything. St. Paul reminds us that nothing can separate us from Christ's love. (See Romans 8:38-39). Therefore, we should look to the future in a trusting spirit.

Our response to the requests of the Blessed Virgin Mary and our openness to the Holy Spirit's guidance and protection will be our help. All things work for good for those who love God (see Romans 8:28), so all prophesied secrets, warnings and chastisements will ultimately lead us to an everlasting experience of love, peace and joy.

I told Mirjana that I wrote this book not to scare people, but to help them to prepare for the secrets, warnings and chastisements so that they don't happen or they are mitigated because the people convert and believe and pray and fast like Our Lady has asked us to do.

She responded, "That's very good that you wrote the book not to scare people. This is important because a mother never scares her children and never gives them a reason to be afraid. She gives them hope and love. Blessed

Mary is not coming to Medjugorje so that we are afraid of the future, but so that we have love and peace in the future with her."

She told me, "The most important thing is to respond to Mary's requests for conversion, faith, prayer and fasting and not to be fearful of any secrets."

I asked Mirjana to comment on Father Petar's statement, "**Everything is closer and closer, God has to do something very quickly.**"

She said, "We can comment in many ways, but, maybe I'll be in front of God tomorrow. I won't have time to wait for secrets, I must change myself today. I always tell the pilgrims, 'Don't talk about secrets, don't think about secrets, think of yourself, think of today, where are you today with God? Because you don't know what you will have tomorrow.'"

Mirjana told Padre Livio, "Not only must we be ready in the future and face the future with great preparation, but we all have to be prepared at all times, because we do not know when God will call us. We must be ready at any moment and live every day in intimate union with God."

The State of the World

In his 1983 letter to Blessed Pope John Paul II, Father Vlasic wrote:

> Mirjana related an apparition she had in 1982 in which Satan appeared to her, and asked Mirjana to renounce the Madonna and to follow him. That way she could be happy in love and in life. He said that following the Virgin, on the contrary, would only lead to suffering. Mirjana rejected him, and immediately the Virgin arrived and Satan disappeared. Then the Blessed Virgin gave her the following message in substance:
> *Excuse me for this, but you must realize that Satan exists. One day he appeared before the throne of God and asked permission to submit the Church to a period of trial. God gave him permission to try the Church for one century.* **This century is under the power of the devil; but when the secrets confided to you come to pass, his power will be destroyed.** *Even now he is beginning to lose his power and has become aggressive. He is destroying marriages, creating divisions among priests and is responsible for obsessions and murder. You must protect yourselves against these things through fasting and prayer, especially community prayer. Carry blessed objects with you. Put them in your house, and restore the use of holy water.*

Mirjana told Father Vlasic in his interview with her:

> The Virgin told me, God and the devil conversed, and the devil said that people believe in God only when life is good for them.

When things turn bad, they cease to believe in God. Then people blame God, or act as if He does not exist.

God therefore, allowed the devil one century in which to exercise an extended power over the world, and the devil chose the twentieth century. Today, as we see all around us, everyone is dissatisfied; they cannot abide each other. Examples are the number of divorces and abortions. All this, Our Lady said, is the work of the devil. . . .

The devil is not in them, but they're under the influence of the devil, although he enters into some of them. To prevent this, at least to some extent, Our Lady said we need communal prayer, family prayer. She stressed the need for family prayer most of all. Also, every family should have at least one sacred object in the house, and houses should be blessed regularly. . . .

[The devil is especially active today] through people of weak character, who are divided within themselves. Such people are everywhere, and they are the easiest for the devil to enter. But he also enters the lives of strong believers. . . .

Mirjana continued with her interview with Father Vlasic in 1983, "Nobody believes — hardly anybody. For example, Our Lady told me that the faith in Germany, Switzerland, and Austria is very weak. The people in those countries model themselves on their priests, and if the priests are not good examples, the people fall away and believe there is no God. . . . You know very well that **the situation of the world is horrible**. There are wars in every part of the world. The situation is very tense. . . . The world has become very evil. It cares about faith very little."

Father Svetozar wrote that Mirjana once said, "God cannot take it anymore!" She told Father Vlasic, "Nowadays, people curse God, Jesus Christ, His Mother, His Father, day in and day out, habitually. Besides, people have fallen into very evil ways, so that they live in evil routinely. It's no wonder that God is at the end of His patience."

Here Mirjana is applying human limitations to God, but she makes her point of how she sees the state of the world in relation to Mary's messages to her. Mary herself said, *"Go on the streets of the city, count those who glorify God and those who offend Him. God can no longer endure that."* (November 11, 1982).

In the third millennium we are experiencing cataclysmic events. The state of the world is worse than it was at the time of the Great Flood. There are great evils that the world has never experienced to this extent before, such as the dissolution of the family through no-fault divorce and same-sex unions; anti-life evils such as contraception, abortion, embryonic experimentation, euthanasia and homosexuality; sex trade and drug trade and addictions; unjust wars, genocides, terrorism, ecological destruction and business and political corruption.

Never has God been more disbelieved, ignored, disobeyed and blasphemed. Many people live as if God does not exist. Many people are their own gods believing and doing whatever they want. Many people are self-absorbed materialists and many seek only money, glory and power. Few people seek to know, love and serve God and to be eternally happy with Him in heaven. The world is becoming more worldly and less godly. Mirjana told Father Vlasic that the greatest danger to mankind is "godlessness. Nobody believes — hardly anybody."

On January 8, 2009, Pope Emeritus Benedict XVI addressed representatives of the 177 countries which have diplomatic relations with the Vatican. This was his "State of the World" address. He said, "**Today more than in the past, our future is at stake, as well as the fate of our planet and its inhabitants,** especially the younger generation which is inheriting a severely compromised economic system and social fabric."

In a later interview with journalist Peter Seewald, the Pope said, "There are of course signs that frighten us, that worry us. But there are also other signs with which we can connect and which give us hope. We have indeed spoken at length already about the scenario of terror and danger." . . .

The Pope then referred to the drug trade and sex tourism and continued, "You see, man strives for eternal joy; he would like pleasure in the extreme, would like what is eternal. But when there is no God, it is not granted to him and it cannot be. Then he himself must now create something that is fictitious, a false eternity."

"This is a sign of the times," he continued, "that should be an urgent challenge to us, especially as Christians. We have to show — and also live this accordingly — that the eternity man needs can come only from God. That **God is the first thing necessary in order to be able to withstand the afflictions of this time.** That we must mobilize, so to speak, all the powers of the soul and of the good so that a genuine coin can stand up against the false coin — and in this way the cycle of evil can be broken and stopped."

"The important thing . . . ," the Pope continued, "is that a need for healing exists, that man can understand again somehow what redemption means. Man recognizes that if God is not there, existence becomes sick and man cannot survive like that. That he needs an answer that he himself cannot give. In that respect this time is a time of Advent that also offers much that is good. The great communication, for example, that we have today can lead, on the one hand, to complete depersonalization. Then one is just swimming in a sea of communication and no longer encounters persons at all. But, on the other hand, it can also be an opportunity. For instance, to become aware of one another, to encounter one another, to help each other, to go out of ourselves."

"So it seems to me important not to see only the negative side. While we must be very keenly aware of it, we must also see all the opportunities for good that are there; the hopes, the new possibilities for being human that exist. So as then, finally, to **proclaim the need for change, which cannot happen without an interior conversion.**"

"Part of this conversion is putting God in first place again. That changes everything else. And inquiring about God's words, so as to allow them as realities to shine into one's own life. We must, so to speak, dare again the experiment with God — so as to allow Him to work within our society." (Seewald, Peter. *Light of the World*. Ft. Collins, CO: Ignatius Press, 2010).

In his traditional Christmas greeting to the Roman Curia on December 20, 2010, Pope Emeritus Benedict XVI noted the parallels that exist between our state of the world and the decline of the Roman Empire.

The Pope noted, "There was no power in sight that could put a stop to this decline. All the more insistent, then, was the invocation of the power of God: the plea that he might come and protect his people from all these threats. The disintegration of the key principles of law and of the fundamental moral attitudes underpinning them burst open the dams which until that time had protected peaceful coexistence among peoples."

We see in our world today what the Pope described in the decline of Rome. He said, "The sun was setting over an entire world. Frequent natural disasters further increased this sense of insecurity."

Comparing our world to Rome, the Pope said, "**For all its new hopes and possibilities, our world is at the same time troubled by the sense that moral consensus is collapsing,** consensus without which juridical and political structures cannot function. Consequently the forces mobilized for the defense of such structures seem doomed to failure."

The Pope then paralleled our sleeping faith to the cry of help from the disciples of Jesus in their storm tossed boat. He said, "[Recall] the cry addressed to the Lord who was sleeping in the disciples' storm-tossed boat as it was close to sinking. When His powerful word had calmed the storm, He rebuked the disciples for their little faith (see Matthew 8:26). He wanted to say: it was your faith that was sleeping. He will say the same thing to us. Our faith too is often asleep. Let us ask Him, then, to wake us from the sleep of a faith grown tired, and to restore to that faith the power to move mountains — that is, to order justly the affairs of the world."

"Alexis de Tocqueville, in his day," the Pope continued, "observed that democracy in America had become possible and had worked because there existed a fundamental moral consensus which, transcending individual denominations, united everyone. Only if there is such a consensus on the essentials can constitutions and law function. This fundamental consensus derived from the Christian heritage is at risk wherever its place, the place of moral reasoning, is taken by the purely instrumental rationality of which I spoke earlier. In reality, this makes reason blind to what is essential. To resist this eclipse of reason and to preserve its capacity for seeing the essential, for seeing God and man, for seeing what is good and what is true, is the common interest that must unite all people of good will. **The very future of the world is at stake.**"

In her 1983 interview with Father Vlasic, Mirjana explained that the century given over to Satan was generally the twentieth century, "part of which is in the twentieth century, **until the first secret is unfolded.**" The implication is that Satan's power will be destroyed after the first secret occurs.

Fr. Petar said, "**Everything is closer and closer. Never in the whole world has the situation been so sad and so bad . . . . Never in history have there been so many sinners and unbelievers. We are feeling that something has to happen very quickly. It cannot continue like this much longer. God has to do something very quickly!**"

Fr. Petar gave a long answer to a question about his thoughts when the secrets would be revealed, asked at the Panel Discussion at the Notre Dame Medjugorje Conference on May 27, 2007. He said:

> We are in the process of patiently waiting for when that's going to take place. From the very beginning, Our Lady was preparing Mirjana how she would reveal those secrets. I was present several times on such discussions Our Lady had with Mirjana. I saw she was crying sometimes, and my question was, 'Why are you crying?' She said, 'I am crying because what she's announcing that would take place — it's no good, it's very serious.'
>
> As I look into the situation in which the world is today, I have the feeling that this should take place very soon. The world cannot go on as it is, under the present condition. Something has to take place. Some intervention from heaven has to take place. It appears as though everything is going towards perdition, but we know that for those that love, God works for good in all events, because God can even write in crooked lines the right way.
>
> What I would like to emphasize is what is most important — that we should not look for the time when it would take place,

but put emphasis on: **Are we ready to face it when it does take place?** He who lives the Gospel in accordance to expectations of the Gospel and Christ has nothing to fear. When Jesus comes, such a person will be ready.

When Mary's warnings are revealed, people will ask, "What are we to do?" The answer is the same answer that St. Peter gave to the Jews when they asked the same question after they heard the mighty wind at Pentecost. St. Peter told them, "Repent and be baptized, every one of you, in the name of Jesus Christ for the forgiveness of your sins; and you will receive the gift of the Holy Spirit." (Acts 2:38).

2: How to Prepare for the Secrets

The Blessed Virgin Mary comes to Medjugorje bringing us urgent messages from God. The summary of her messages is that peace can come only from God through conversion and faith, maintained by the sacraments (especially Confession and the Eucharist), prayer and fasting, reading Scripture and the use of sacramentals.

All adults have the capacity to know that God exists. The sin of the world lies in that there is no interest or time for God. Mary comes to tell the world that God exists and that **peace is necessary for the salvation of the world.**

Peace

Mary said, *"I have come here as Queen of Peace to tell the world that peace is necessary for the salvation of the world. In God, one finds true joy from which true peace is derived."* (June 16, 1983).

She also said, *"Jesus is the King of Peace, and only He can give you the peace that you seek."* (December 25, 1995).

Mirjana told Father Vlasic that Mary introduced herself as the Queen of Peace because, "the situation of the world is horrible. There are wars in every part of the world. The situation is very tense. Peace is needed — a just and simple peace. First, peace in the soul. If a person has it in his soul, he is surrounded by it. Peace comes as result of faith in God and surrender to Him as a consequence of prayer, penance, and fasting."

Peace is the natural desire of every human heart. However, peace is not obtainable by any human peace program or from money, drugs, power or anything else without Jesus Christ who said, "Without me you can do nothing." (John 15:5).

Jesus said, "**Peace I leave with you; my peace I give to you. Not as the world gives do I give it to you. Do not let your hearts be troubled or afraid.**" (John 15:27). Peace is a gift from God that cannot be earned by our effort, imposed by political effort or gained by any human means whatsoever. As Mary said, only Jesus can give us the peace that we seek.

Blessed Pope John Paul II said, "In the end, peace is not essentially about structures but about people. Certain structures and mechanisms of peace — juridical, political, economic — are of course necessary and do exist, but they have been derived from nothing other than the accumulated wisdom and experience of innumerable gestures of peace made by men and women throughout history who have kept hope and have not given in to discouragement. **Gestures of peace spring from the lives of people who foster peace first of all in their own hearts. They are the work of the heart and of reason in those who are peacemakers** (see Mt 5:9)." (Blessed Pope John Paul II, *Message for the Celebration of the World Day of Peace*, January 1, 2003).

Peace is not merely the absence of external conflict. It is a positive interior quality, which is a gift from Jesus (see John 14:27), beginning in our hearts and flowing like a river to our family, neighbors, friends and society, gathering them all in its current. We seek and yearn for this peace because God has instilled this yearning in us so that we will rest in Him.

St. Augustine said, "You have made us for yourself, O Lord, and our hearts are restless until they rest in you." Only then will we experience God's own peace, which is beyond all understanding. (See Philippians 4:7).

Each of us must truthfully answer the eternal questions, "Who am I?, Why am I? and What is my destiny?" The meaning of being human is that we are dependent creatures of God our Creator, who made us for Himself out of His love for us and gave us great dignity.

The psalmist said, "What are humans that you are mindful of them, mere mortals that you care for them? Yet you have made them little less than a god, crowned them with glory and honor." (Psalm 8:5-6).

We have dignity because we are created in God's image (see Genesis 1:26) with intellect, wills, actions and immortal souls. We are called to know Him, to love Him and to serve Him on earth so that we will have happiness and eternal life with Him in heaven. "He merited for us life by the free shedding of His own blood. In Him God reconciled us (see 2 Corinthians 5:18-19; Colossians 1:20-22) to Himself and among ourselves; from bondage to the devil and sin He delivered us, so that each one of us can say with the Apostle: The Son of God 'loved me and gave Himself up for me. (Galatians 2:20)' ". (Documents of Vatican II, *Pastoral Constitution on the Church in the Modern World*, 22). St. Paul also said, "You have been purchased at a price." (1 Corinthians 20).

Jesus said that eternal life is to know the one, true God, and the one whom He sent, Jesus Himself. (See John 17:3). Those who believe in Him have eternal life. (See 1 John 5:13). We "believe in Him" through faith that He is true God and true man, our Lord and Savior. We humbly submit to all that He revealed as to what we should believe and do, and to the authoritative teaching of the one true Church that He founded.

"The way we may be sure that we know Him is to keep His commandments. Whoever says, 'I know Him,' but does not keep His commandments, is a liar, and the truth is not in him. But whoever keeps His word, the love of God is truly perfected in him. This is the way we may know that we are in union with Him: whoever claims to abide in Him ought to live just as he lived." (1 John 2:1-6). Through this union with Him we become a mysterious new creation and partake of God's own life of grace and truth for all eternity. Jesus Christ fully reveals man to himself and we see our divine destiny to live with Him in eternal life and happiness.

Even without this divine revelation, we can know that God exists by reason alone without faith. God created us as rational animals with mortal material bodies and immortal, immaterial souls with intellects to know the truth, wills to do the good and emotions to appreciate beauty. We come to know this by our reasoning powers alone unaided by God's revelation. "For what can be known about God is evident . . . , because God made it evident. . . . Ever since the creation of the world, His invisible attributes of eternal power and divinity have been able to be understood and perceived in what He has made." (Romans 1:19-20).

As a result, **those who deny God's existence or act as if He does not exist, have no excuse and they do not accord Him glory, as God or give Him thanks. Instead, they become vain in their reasoning, their senseless minds are darkened and they have no peace.** (See Romans 1:20-21). "They exchanged the truth of God for a lie and revered and worshiped the creature rather than the Creator." (Romans 1:25). We see this in our own world today.

Not only can we know the truth of God's existence by our unaided reason, we can also know His will to do good and avoid evil and His law to love God and our neighbor. "In the depths of his conscience, man detects a law which he does not impose upon himself, but which holds him to obedience. Always summoning him to love good and avoid evil, the voice of conscience when necessary speaks to his heart: do this, shun that. For man has in his heart a law written by God; to obey it is the very dignity of man; according to it he will be judged. (See Romans 2:15-16). Conscience is the most secret core and sanctuary of a man. There he is alone with God, whose voice echoes in his depths. In a wonderful manner conscience reveals that law which is fulfilled by love of God and neighbor. (See Matthew 22:37-40; Galatians 5:14)." (Documents of Vatican II, *Pastoral Constitution on the Church in the Modern World*, 16).

Those who deny God, who do not listen to His voice and disobey His law are handed over by Him "to their undiscerning mind to do what is improper." (Romans 1: 28). And what do the deniers of God do that is improper? They degrade their bodies through lust and unnatural homosexual relations. (Romans 1: 24-27). "They are filled with every form of wickedness, evil, greed, and malice; full of envy, murder, rivalry, treachery, and spite. They are gossips and scandalmongers and they hate God. They are insolent, haughty, boastful, ingenious in their wickedness, and rebellious toward their parents. They are senseless, faithless, heartless, ruthless. Although they know the just decree of God that all who practice such things deserve death, they not only do them but give approval to those who practice them." (Romans 1:29-32).

They lose the peace of God and freely choose eternal death. "We know that the judgment of God on those who do such things is true." (Romans 2:2). "[He] will repay everyone according to his works: eternal life to those who seek glory, honor, and immortality through perseverance in good works, but wrath and fury to those who selfishly disobey the truth and obey wickedness." (Romans 2:6-8).

On the contrary, **those who conform their wills to the will of God through conversion, faith, prayer and fasting, and keep His Commandments have a clear conscience and the gift of His peace.**

Pope Emeritus Benedict XVI recognized that peace is a gift from God alone and is built and preserved only when human beings can freely seek and serve Him in their hearts, in their lives and in their relationships with others. He said:

> The truth, goodness, happiness and abundant life which each man and woman consciously or unconsciously seeks are given to us by God. In longing for these gifts, each person is seeking his Creator, for "God alone responds to the yearning present in the heart of every man and woman" (Post-Synodal Apostolic Exhortation *Verbum Domini*, 23). Humanity throughout history, in its beliefs and rituals, demonstrates a constant search for God and "these forms of religious expression are so universal that one may well call man a religious being." (*Catechism of the Catholic Church*, 28). The religious dimension is an undeniable and irrepressible feature of man's being and acting, the measure of the fulfilment of his destiny and of the building up of the community to which he belongs. Consequently, when the individual himself or those around him neglect or deny this fundamental dimension, imbalances and conflicts arise at all levels, both personal and interpersonal. This primary and basic truth is the reason why, in this year's Message for World Day of Peace, I identified religious freedom as the fundamental path to peace. Peace is built and preserved only when human beings can freely seek and serve God

in their hearts, in their lives and in their relationships with others." (Pope Emeritus Benedict XVI, *New Year Address to Diplomatic Corps,* January 10, 2011).

When people neglect these eternal truths and the call to peace, conflicts arise. Fr. Svetozar Kraljevic wrote in *The Apparitions of Our Lady at Medjugorje,* "The world was called to peace, but it went to war [the Yugoslavian Civil War]. Precisely ten years after Mary appeared, the first explosions of war were heard. We wonder what we shall miss again. And what shall take place in the future?"

The future is in the secrets. We should respond now to Mary's request for peace and not to miss it again. We can possess anything in this world, but if we do not have peace, we have nothing. The only true peace is the one that Jesus gives. However, this **peace is not obtainable, as Mary said, unless we repent (convert), believe (have faith), reconcile with God and one another (go to Confession), pray (especially the Rosary) and fast.**

The angels greeted the shepherds of Bethlehem and said, "Glory to God in the highest, and on earth peace among men with whom He is pleased." (Luke 2: 14). Pope Emeritus Benedict XVI said, "The angel's greeting to the shepherds on the night of Christ's birth in Bethlehem reveals an unbreakable link between the relationship of men and women with God and their own mutual relationships. **Peace on earth cannot be found without reconciliation with God, without harmony between heaven and earth."** (Pope Emeritus Benedict XVI, *Address to the Roman Curia,* December 22, 2006).

Conversion

Mirjana told Father Vlasic, "Our Lady said people should prepare themselves spiritually, be ready, and not panic; be reconciled in their souls. They should be ready for the worst, to die tomorrow. They should accept God now so that they will not be afraid. They should accept God, and everything else. No one accepts death easily, but they can be at peace in their souls if they are believers. If they are committed to God, He will accept them. This means total conversion and surrender to God. I say to all people: **Convert! — the same as she said, 'Convert while there is time!' "**

"Do not abandon God and your faith. Abandon everything else, but not that!" she continued. "I ask priests to help their people, because priests can cause them to reject their faith. After a man has been ordained, he must really be a priest, bring people to the Church. The most important point is that the people convert and pray." **Each of us must answer the question that God asked Fred Beretta before his Miracle on the Hudson, "Will you reconcile and trust? You must choose."**

Conversion is a total interior change of heart which proceeds from our repentance, reconciliation and the submission of our wills to seek first the kingdom of God. (See Matthew 3:2; 6:33). We turn from following our own wills to follow the will of God and from our values to His and abandon in trust everything that takes us away from Him.

The call of the prophets is to repent, meaning to convert, to turn to God and to change our ways and be reconciled with Him and one another. Mary's first appearance at Medjugorje was on the Feast of St. John the Baptist. This is significant since he was the last of the prophets before Jesus. Between them, all righteousness was fulfilled. (See Matthew 3:15). They both gave the same call, "**Repent, for the kingdom of heaven is at hand.**" (Matthew 3:2; 4:17).

Jesus has sent His mother to Medjugorje for the same reason that He sent St. Paul to the pagans — "To open their eyes, so that they may turn from darkness to light, from the dominion of Satan to God, and receive, through faith in me, forgiveness of their sins and a share in the inheritance of the sanctified." (Acts 26:18).

The prophet Ezekiel spoke in God's name and said, "As I live, says the Lord God, I swear I take no pleasure in the death of the wicked man, but in the wicked man's conversion, that he may live." (Ezekiel 33:10-11).

The prophet Jeremiah called the Israelites to conversion and said, "Cleanse your heart of evil." (Jeremiah 4:14). Jesus said, "For from the heart come evil thoughts, murder, adultery, unchastity, theft, false witness, blasphemy. These are what defile a person." (Matthew 15:19-20).

Conversion consists of a radical reformation of our lives and hearts by which we acknowledge and confess our sins, turn from the values of the world to those of Jesus Christ and believe and accept the Gospel message and His person as the Son of God and our personal Lord and Savior. Through conversion, we turn from sin and selfishness, submit to Jesus as Lord of our minds and hearts and change our ways of thinking and acting. True repentance requires a contrite heart (see Psalm 51:17) and sorrow for sin and a firm purpose to amend our lives and to avoid the near of occasions of sin in the future.

One of the greatest conversion stories of all time is that of Saul of Tarsus who became St. Paul. He testified how he first opposed the Gospel and persecuted Christians, but was converted when Christ appeared to him on the road to Damascus. (See Acts 22:3-16). Paul's encounter with the person of Christ radically changed his life and opened his eyes to the truth of the Gospel. Pope Emeritus Benedict XVI reflected on the significance of Paul's conversion for the whole Christian people:

Paul's conversion matured in his encounter with the Risen Christ; it was this encounter that radically changed his life. What happened to him on the road to Damascus is what Jesus asks in today's Gospel: Saul is converted because, thanks to the divine light, "he has believed in the Gospel." In this consists his and our conversion: in believing in Jesus dead and risen and in opening to the illumination of His divine grace. In that moment Saul understood that his salvation did not depend on good works fulfilled according to the law, but on the fact that Jesus died also for him the persecutor and has risen. This truth by which every Christian life is enlightened thanks to Baptism completely overturns our way of life. To be converted means, also for each one of us, to believe that Jesus "has given himself for me", dying on the Cross (see Galatians 2: 20) and, risen, lives with me and in me. Entrusting myself to the power of His forgiveness, letting myself be taken by His hand, I can come out of the quicksands of pride and sin, of deceit and sadness, of selfishness and of every false security, to know and live the richness of His love. (Pope Emeritus Benedict XVI, January 25, 2009).

God's grace brings pardon and absolution for our sins, especially through the sacrament of Confession, by which we are reconciled to God and one another and become His friends and the friends of one another. This causes, through His grace, an interior transformation producing fruits of prayer, self-denial and charity. (See Acts 26:20). This is the foundation of all Christianity. (See Hebrews 6:1-2). Mary especially recommended the monthly reception of the sacrament of Confession. (See Chapter 5 for How to Make a Good Confession).

Faith

Mirjana told Father Vlasic, "Evil things will happen because the world has become very evil. It cares about faith very little."

Mary said, *"Faith is a vital element but one cannot compel a person to believe.* **Faith is the foundation from which everything flows."** (November 31, 1981).

Jesus said, "This is the work of God: have faith in the one He sent." (John 6:29). "Without faith, it is impossible to please Him." (Hebrews 11:6).

Before His ascension to heaven, Jesus appeared to His apostles and said, "Go into the whole world and proclaim the Gospel to every creature. **Whoever believes and is baptized will be saved; whoever does not believe will be condemned.**" (Mark 16:15-18).

Faith is the submission of our intellect and will to God's revelation, in particular to the good news of the new covenant of eternal salvation through the forgiveness of our sins. (See Mark 1:15; Hebrews 9:26; Romans 3:24-26). "[Jesus Christ] is mediator of a new covenant: since a death has taken place for deliverance from transgressions under the first covenant, those who are called may receive the promised eternal inheritance." (Hebrews 9:15). We believe God's promises because He is all-good and will not deceive us.

Faith is not contrary to reason but a belief in the person and message of Jesus Christ as a living witness accredited by God through His works (see Matthew 11:2-6; John 5:36; John 10:25, 37; John 14:11); His character (see John 8:46-59); His doctrine (see John 7:16-17) and confirmed in His resurrection (See Romans 1:4). Faith is both preceded and assisted by God's grace.

After John the Baptist was put in prison, Jesus went into the Galilee region of Israel and proclaimed the good news of God. He said, "The time has come. The kingdom of God is near. Repent and believe the good news!" (Mark 1:14-15). So, **in addition to conversion (repentance) we must *believe* His good news.**

We should believe the proclamation of Jesus, because He demonstrated that "the kingdom of God was not a matter of talk, but of power." (1 Corinthians 4:20). "He went around all of Galilee, teaching in their synagogues, proclaiming the gospel of the kingdom, and curing every disease and illness among the people. His fame spread to all of Syria, and they brought to Him all who were sick with various diseases and racked with pain, those who were possessed, lunatics, and paralytics, and He cured them." (Matthew 4:23-24).

The Kingdom of God. The good news (Gospel) that Jesus proclaimed, was that the kingdom of God was near. This kingdom is not a geographical area on the earth, like Israel. Moreover, it is not an historical event which is fixed in time, like the kingdom of King Herod.

The kingdom of God is the same as the kingdom of heaven. It is eternal life and its beginning may be enjoyed now. (See Matthew 25:34, 46; John 3:15). "For God so loved the world that he gave His only Son, so that everyone who believes in Him might not perish but might have eternal life." (John 3:16).

The kingdom of God is also the person of Christ Himself and His Church. The members of His kingdom are the children of God who enter it through conversion, faith, baptism and the forgiveness of sins, and the acceptance of the person of Jesus Christ and the teachings of His Church, which is His kingdom on earth. The final realization of His kingdom will occur in the glory of His second coming. (See Matthew 24:26-31). The kingdom of God has come (see Luke 11:20; Matthew 4:17) and will come (see Luke 9:27), for which we are to pray (see Matthew 6:10).

The kingdom of God is the reign of God and His sovereignty and authority over all peoples and nations forever. (See Psalm 103:19; Zechariah 14:9, 16; Revelation 15:4). His kingdom is universal and everlasting (see Daniel 4:3); it is meant for all humankind, and all people are called to become members of it. It is full of glory, power, and splendor (see Psalm 145:11-13). It is "righteousness, peace and joy in the Holy Spirit." (Romans 14: 17).

At one and the same time, the kingdom of God has arrived and is arriving towards a perfect realization. Its presence is not two events but two stages of the same event, one of which is here while the other is an object of hope and prayer. The kingdom of God is inaugurated in Jesus Christ Himself. (See Matthew 12:25-28; Vatican II, *Dogmatic Constitution on the Church*, 5) and moves towards its perfect realization by means of His Church. (See Matthew 10:7, 16:19). Jesus revealed the kingdom of God by His intervention into the world with His teachings, miracles, and exorcisms, which radically overthrew the kingdom of Satan. (See Mark 3:27).

This kingdom reveals itself through Jesus to all people who should submit to it in faith. The kingdom comes to us individually as an offer of pardon to be freely accepted by reforming our lives and believing in and surrendering to the sovereignty of God in the person of Jesus Christ. Those who fail to reform must face His judgment. (See Matthew 11:20-24).

The blessings of the kingdom to those who submit to it are the forgiveness of their sins (see Mark 2:5); God's provident care (see Matthew 6:33); and the gift of God's Holy Spirit (see Acts 2:38). In the future, God "will wipe every tear from their eyes, and there shall be no more death or mourning, wailing or pain," (Revelation 21:4) "and they shall reign forever and ever." (Revelation 22:5).

Baptism. We enter the kingdom of God through Baptism. When the mighty noisy wind of Pentecost blew in Jerusalem in 33 A.D., the Jews there knew that they had experienced a supernatural sign. When the first warning comes, three days after its announcement from Medjugorje, the world will know that it experienced a fulfilled prophecy. Then, like the Jews in Jerusalem, almost 2000 years ago, the people will say, "What are we to do?" (Acts 2:37).

The answer to that question today is the same answer that St. Peter gave to the Jews, "Repent and be baptized, every one of you, in the name of Jesus Christ for the forgiveness of your sins; and you will receive the gift of the Holy Spirit." (Acts 2:38).

Conversion and faith are culminated in the sacrament of Baptism. Those who have converted but are unbaptized, must be baptized. Jesus told

Nicodemus, "Amen, Amen, I say to you, no one can enter the kingdom of God without being born of water and Spirit." (John 3:5). All of the faithful must be baptized and receive the sacraments of Confession, Eucharist and Confirmation.

Baptism is the sign and the reality of being cleansed from sin. The unbaptized should be prepared for this and the other sacraments through the Catholic Church's Rite of Christian Initiation for Adults (RCIA). Conversion is not a single act, we are all in need of continual conversion and that's why Mary asks us to receive the sacrament of Confession monthly.

In the sacrament of Baptism, we die to sin and our old life and rise to a new life in Jesus Christ in the hopes of our rising from the dead to have eternal life in glory with Him. St. Gregory of Nazianzus, a seventh century Church Father, tells us, "Let us be buried with Christ by Baptism to rise with Him; let us go down with Him to be raised with Him; and let us rise with Him to be glorified with Him."

Pope Emeritus Benedict XVI said, "I would like to encourage all of the faithful to rediscover the beauty of being baptized and belonging to the great family of God and to giving a joyous witness to their own faith so that they might bear the fruits of goodness and concord."

He noted how each baptized person "acquires the character of son from the name Christian, indisputable sign that the Holy Spirit brings man to be born 'again' from the womb of the Church." He continued, "Blessed Anotonio Rosmini says that 'the baptized person undergoes a secret but most powerful operation by which he is raised up to the supernatural order, he is placed in communication with God.'" (Pope Emeritus Benedict XVI, January 9, 2011).

"Therefore the Church announces the good tidings of salvation [being saved from eternal death and sin] to those who do not believe, so that all men may know the true God and Jesus Christ whom He has sent, and may be converted from their ways, doing penance. (See John 17:3; Luke 24:27; Acts 2:38). To believers also the Church must ever preach faith and penance. . . ." (*Documents of Vatican II*, the Constitution of the Sacred Liturgy, 9).

Our response to hearing the good tidings of salvation is governed by the Second Vatican Council, which stated:

> "The obedience of faith" (Romans 16:26; 2 Corinthians 10:5-6) is to be given to God who reveals, an obedience by which man commits his whole self freely to God, offering "the full submission of intellect and will to God who reveals" and freely assenting to the truth revealed by Him. (*Documents of Vatican II*, the Dogmatic Constitution on Divine Revelation, 1:5).

Prayer and Fasting

Prayer and fasting maintain conversion and faith which are inextricably linked in the chain of peace. Prayer should calmly and peacefully proceed from an interior desire for union with God without preoccupation to distractions.

Mary said, *"Pray with great meditation. Do not look at your watch all the time, but allow yourself to be led by the grace of God. Do not concern yourself too much with the things of this world, but entrust all that in prayer to our heavenly Father. If one is preoccupied, he will not be able to pray well because internal security is lacking."* (June 16, 1983).

According to Father Svetozar, a priest asked the visionaries to ask Mary whether we should pray to Jesus or to her. Mary responded, *"Pray to Jesus. I am His mother, and I intercede with Him, but say all your prayers to Jesus. I will help you pray, but the strength of your prayers is more important."*

Mirjana told Father Vlasic, "**When we pray, we pray to God. In return, we receive peace of soul, tranquility. We have opened our hearts to God, so that God can enter and when we have God in our heart and soul, we cannot cause evil to anybody.** We will not curse — do anything evil. We will do good. We also have to pray for others. For example, **I always pray for nonbelievers, because they do not know what is missing in their lives. They have no idea of how much they may have to suffer later.** I pray that God will convert them, that He will give them a sign, that He will open their souls so that they can accept the faith."

"Much can be done through prayer and fasting," Mirjana continued. "Our Lady has said that **prayer can stop wars and prevent catastrophes. Prayer and fasting!** Of course prayer can help a struggling human who does not accept God and religion. Moreover, we are obliged to pray that such a person's heart will be opened. Again, I talk to many nonbelievers in Sarajevo and try to explain things to them so that they will gain a least a little understanding. Sometimes, it is not their fault; they received no religious training when they were young. Or later, when they abandoned their faith, no one tried to help them. I pray that God will open such hearts."

Mirjana told Father Vlasic how she prayed. "I pray the Rosary and I pray for an hour or two, depending on how much time I have. But usually never less than one hour. I pray that God will give me the strength of soul that I can again think and behave normally. I also pray for unbelievers, for their conversion. And for the secrets.... When I pray, something comes to me, because I immerse myself in prayer. Then it's as if I'm speaking with someone. I express things in the way I think they should be said, all the while talking to God. Then I go back to saying the regular kind of prayers. Then I pray again in my own words. I say all this out loud...."

"If we pray for a particular need," Mirjana continued, "we should emphasize exactly that: 'Dear God, I'm praying to be healed of my illness.' Pray like that. But pray from your heart, from the bottom of your soul, with feeling. It does not have to be a 'regular' prayer, but a conversation with God. 'God, you see my suffering. You know how I am. I'm not complaining, my cross is not too difficult to bear; but I would like to be on my feet again so that I can move around in the world.' Like that: conversation, then prayer."

Mirjana concluded, "I believe that sick people should speak and pray to God for one hour every day, intimately. I'm sure it would restore their souls and that God would grant them grace. Our Lady always recommended faith, prayer, and penance. She never mentioned anything special for anybody, whether they were sick or healthy. But, she said we should direct our prayers: 'I am praying for such – and – such.' And we should pray with concentration, not race through the words of Our Father. The main thing is not to say the words of a prayer, but to feel them."

In an interview at Medjugorje on October 3, 2009, Mirjana said, "We can always pray better and we grow in that. I always recommend to everybody, do not waste your time judging yourself in your own prayer. Pray and God will help you. Sometimes you just feel like you prayed great, sometimes not, but Our Lady always offers her hand as mother and she will always raise you up. Do not forget, God is love and He loves you and He knows you and it is important that you desire to come closer to Him and He will help you."

Mirjana continued, "Our Lady asks us to pray from the heart. I understand that to mean that every word that comes out of my mouth would pass through my heart first. So, when I say, 'Hail Mary,' then I truly greet Mary with my heart. When I say, 'full of grace,' then I feel within myself how much grace Our Lady gives me and to everyone. It is never a repetition for me because I always feel some new, different things when I pray the Hail Mary."

"For example," she continued, "when I reflect that Our Lady was assumed into heaven, I think about her. I talk with her. I ask her about how she felt and all that she thought. I do not see her. I do not hear her, but just with my heart. Try that. If your thoughts still wander, put the Rosary aside and talk with Our Lady and tell her why, what your burden is and why you can't be still and pray. Whatever you have in your heart, give it to her."

Mirjana told me that she wanted "to ask everybody to **pray for those who do not recognize the love of God yet**. Because when we pray for them, we pray for us, for our future, because who of us can say, 'I am a good believer, I'm doing everything that God wants'? And when we pray for them, we pray for us."

Jesus is a model for prayer whom we should imitate. He often prayed all night long, even to the point of sweating blood. (See Luke 22:44). He condemned any prayer that is said for the sake of notice. (See Matthew 6:5). He remarked upon the brief petition for pardon uttered by the tax collector as the prayer that justifies a man. (See Luke 18:10). In our prayer, we should recognize the unredeemed sin within us, offer it to Jesus for His redemption and continually yearn to be closer to God. The more we pray, the more we are conformed to the mind of Christ and live as a child of the Father.

Mary especially recommended the reading of Scripture, the Rosary, the use of sacramentals and the best prayer, the celebration of the Eucharistic liturgy. (See Chapter 5 for How to Read Scripture, How to Pray, How to Pray the Rosary, How to Celebrate The Eucharist and How to Use Sacramentals).

Pope Emeritus Benedict XVI said, "**As believers, we are convinced that prayer is a true force. It opens the world to God: We are convinced that God listens and that he can act in history.** I think that if millions of people — believers — would pray, it could really be a force that could influence and contribute to the advancement of peace." (Pope Emeritus Benedict XVI, Aboard the Papal Plane, May 8, 2009).

Mary asked us to pray with her and to pray as much as possible, including the Rosary every day. She said, "*In addition, I want them to fast on Wednesdays and Fridays.*" (August 14, 1984).

Mirjana told Father Vlasic, "Sick people do not have to fast. If they do not fast, it is not a sin for them. They can do another good deed instead. For those who are able to fast, it is not enough that they do a good deed instead. We did not discuss fasting except on bread and water. But probably she meant we should fast only on bread and water. Everyone who wants to receive something from God or have God's help, must fast."

In her interview at Medjugorje on October 3, 2009, Mirjana said, "When I'm fasting, I'm proving to myself that I am the boss of my own body and that I can do for God anything I want, that nothing can stop me. And with this fasting, I'm showing God that with this little, I am ready to do even more if that is what He desires. Through fasting my prayer is stronger. I feel closer to Him."

Jesus is also a model person for fasting. He fasted in the desert for 40 days after His Baptism. (See Luke 4:2). He said that certain demons could not be cast out except through prayer and fasting. (Matthew 17:21; Mark 9:29). Jesus condemned the appearance of self-denial. (See Matthew 6: 16-18). External fasting without interior love of God and neighbor are really works for one's self. True fasting that delights the Lord involves more of charity than self-denial. (See Isaiah 58:6-7; Matthew 9:13).

Mary especially recommended as "the best fast", fasting on bread and water on Wednesdays and Fridays. We fast on these days because Wednesday is the day that Judas made the arrangements to betray Jesus and Friday is the day that they crucified Him. (See Chapter 5 for How to Fast).

Mary asked for all of this prayer and fasting in order to maintain our peace and to mitigate worldly chastisements. She makes these requests as a mother concerned for our temporal and eternal welfare, aware of the evil rampant in the world and warning us of chastisements. She said, "***Through fasting and prayer one can stop wars, one can suspend the natural laws of nature.***" (July 21, 1982).

The world is involved in a supernatural battle between the forces of good and evil. Only supernatural weapons can be effective in such a battle. St. Paul tells us to "put on the armor of God so that you may be able to stand firm against the tactics of the devil. Our battle is not against human forces but against the principalities and powers, the rulers of this world of darkness, the evil spirits in regions above." (Ephesians 6:11-12).

The supernatural weapons requested by Mary at Medjugorje are conversion and faith, maintained by prayer and fasting. Prayer and fasting will help to bring about peace. Mary said that peace is necessary for the salvation of the world and that she is the Queen of Peace.

Total Consecration to Jesus through Mary

Mary also asked us at Medjugorje to consecrate ourselves to her Immaculate Heart. By this consecration we totally entrust and dedicate ourselves to Jesus through Mary as our Mediatrix. This is the consecration that Blessed Pope John Paul II made to her as the Mediatrix of All Graces and took as his motto *Totus Tuus (Totally Yours)*. He wrote:

> This role of Mary, [as the Mediatrix of All Graces] totally grounded in that of Christ and radically subordinated to it, "in no way obscures or diminishes the unique mediation of Christ, but rather shows its power." This is the luminous principle expressed by the Second Vatican Council which I have so powerfully experienced in my own life and have made the basis of my episcopal motto: *Totus Tuus (Totally Yours)*. The motto is of course inspired by the teaching of Saint Louis Marie Grignion de Montfort, who explained in the following words Mary's role in the process of our configuration to Christ: "Our entire perfection consists in being conformed, united and consecrated to Jesus Christ. Hence the

most perfect of all devotions is undoubtedly that which conforms, unites and consecrates us most perfectly to Jesus Christ. Now, since Mary is of all creatures the one most conformed to Jesus Christ, it follows that **among all devotions that which most consecrates and conforms a soul to our Lord is devotion to Mary, His holy mother, and that the more a soul is consecrated to her the more will it be consecrated to Jesus Christ.**" (Blessed Pope John Paul II, Apostolic Letter, *The Rosary of the Virgin Mary*, 2002, 1:15).

The Pope referred to St. Louis de Montfort who wrote the book *True Devotion to Mary*, in which he teaches total consecration to Jesus through Mary as a means of renewing our baptismal promises. By this total consecration, we renounce Satan, his pomps and works and permanently dedicate ourselves to Jesus through Mary, giving her our bodies and souls, our goods and even the merits of our good works for her disposition according to her will. (See Chapter 5 for How to Make The Total Consecration.)

An understanding of the role of the Blessed Virgin Mary in God's plan of salvation will help us to respond to her requests.

3: The Role of the Blessed Virgin Mary in God's Plan of Salvation

The Blessed Virgin Mary appeared in Mexico on December 9, 1531. She identified herself as Our Lady of Guadalupe and told St. Juan Diego:

> *Know for certain, dearest of my sons, that I am the perfect and perpetual Virgin Mary, mother of the one true God, through whom everything lives, the Lord of all things near and far, the Master of heaven and earth. I ardently desire that a sacred house be built here for me where I will show Him, I will exalt Him and make Him manifest, I will give Him to the people and offer all my love, my compassion, my help and my protection. I am your merciful mother, the merciful mother of all who live united in this land, and of all mankind, of all those who love me, of those who cry to me, of those who have confidence in me. Here I will hear their weeping and their sorrows, and I will remedy and alleviate their sufferings, necessities and misfortunes.*

These words show **that Mary's role in God's plan of salvation as our merciful mother is to manifest her Son Jesus to us and to bring us her help and protection as a mediatrix with her Son. God's plan of salvation is to bring all creation under the final rule of Christ.** (See Ephesians 1:10). "In subjecting all things to Him, God left nothing unsubjected. At present we do not see all things thus subject, but we do see Jesus crowned with glory and honor because He suffered death." (Hebrews 2:8 -9).

God the Father chose us in Christ to be His adopted sons and to be holy and blameless in His sight through Christ's redemption. His redemption bought back for us the gifts of the supernatural life of grace and heaven which were lost by the original sin of Adam and Eve. Our salvation is a fruit of this and by His passion and death, we have eternal salvation in heaven through faith and the forgiveness of our sins. (See Ephesians 1:4-7; 2:8). The Father's creation is redeemed by the Son and is made holy by the Spirit's sanctification by which we have our salvation which is eternal life through the forgiveness of our sins.

Pope Paul VI said that the Blessed Virgin Mary "has a most singular 'role in the mystery of the incarnate Word and of the mystical body,' that is to say, in the 'economy of salvation' …". (Encyclical Letter, *Signum Magnum, (The Great Sign),* Pope Paul VI, May 13, 1967).

St. Louis de Montfort said that "it was through Mary that the salvation of the world was begun, and it is through Mary that it must be consummated." (*True Devotion to Mary,* 49).

Pope Paul VI said, "… **the Blessed Virgin Mary, after participating in the redeeming sacrifice of the Son … now continues to fulfill from heaven her maternal function as the cooperator in the birth and development of divine life in the individual souls of redeemed men. This is a most consoling truth, which, by the free consent of God the All-Wise, is an integrating part of the mystery of human salvation; therefore it must be held as faith by all Christians."** (Encyclical Letter, *Signum Magnum, (The Great Sign),* Pope Paul VI, May 13, 1967).

Mary's central role in the divine plan of our salvation is to cooperate in the redemption accomplished by her Son Jesus. On earth she cooperated with Him. In heaven she has cooperated with Him from the time of her Assumption and Coronation. She will continue to cooperate with Him as the Mediatrix of All Graces until God is all in all. (See 1 Corinthians 15:28). All graces that Jesus merited by His passion and death are mediated to us by the intercession and dispensation of Mary.

As she was the mother of Jesus in natural life (the order of nature) so, too, is she the mother of the baptized in supernatural life (the order of grace). As she brought forth Jesus at Bethlehem, so she brings Him forth again in receptive human hearts through the mediation of her Immaculate Heart until He will reign in all hearts with her by the triumph of her Immaculate Heart in the world. This will be the fulfillment of St. Louis' prophecy that the consummation of the salvation of the world will be through Mary.

Her role is carried out throughout the history of the world amidst constant battle with Satan and his many followers, whose pride and disobedience will ultimately be defeated through her and her Son and the humility and obedience of their followers.

We can see this central role of Mary through the events of the Fall of the angels, the Fall of man and the mysteries of her life.

The Fallen Angels

In the beginning of time, God created heaven and earth, and angels as pure spirits. (See Colossians 1:16). They were created as immortal beings out of the goodness of God for His glorification. (See Hebrews 2:10). He endowed them with grace, but they were subjected to a moral testing. God gave them a one-time fundamental option to acknowledge Him as their maker and Lord and to choose to serve Him or not.

The good angels who passed the test were rewarded with the blessedness of heaven. (See Matthew 18:10). Satan (meaning Adversary) and the other angels, who did not pass the test through their own sin, fell from heaven and were eternally damned (see 2 Peter 2:4; Jude 6), even though they knew that such would be the consequence of their disobedience! One unrepented mortal sin committed by us can have the same result.

On April 14, 1982, Mirjana had a vision while she was waiting for Mary to appear. Satan arrived disguised as Mary. Mirjana said, "He was ugly, horribly ugly. You cannot even imagine how ugly, he almost killed me with his gaze, I almost fainted. He then told me, 'You must leave God and Mary because they will make you suffer, come with me and I will make you happy in love and life.' My heart echoed – No, no, no!"

"Then Satan went away and Mary came and she said to me:"

> I am sorry for this, but you must know that Satan exists. One day, he presented himself before the throne of God and asked permission to try the Church for a period of time. God permitted him to try it during one century but said, 'You will not destroy Her.' **This century is under the power of the devil, but when the secrets which have been confided to you have been fulfilled, his power will be destroyed.** Satan has become aggressive because he is losing his power. He is breaking up marriages, causing quarrels amongst priests, obsessing people, even killing them. Therefore, protect yourselves by prayer, fasting and, above all, community prayer. Renew the use of holy water, wear blessed and holy objects and put them in your homes.

We should also pray to our Guardian angels and pray the prayer of St. Michael the Archangel. (See Appendix A). This was composed by Pope Leo XIII, in the late nineteenth century when he saw in a vision the satanic evil to come. The angels protect us and help us towards our salvation.

The Fall of Man

God created Adam and Eve out of His goodness and for His glory with the gifts of immortality and grace. These gifts were not just for themselves, but for transmission to the whole human race. These gifts were lost by their original sin of disobedience to God's command through the temptation of Satan. (See Genesis 2:17, 3:1 and following). As a result of this, they, and all of us, became subject to suffering, sin, death and the power of Satan. (See Genesis 3:15 and following).

The disobedience of the fallen angels and of Adam and Eve prompted the Protogospel (the first good news), whereby God set up an irreconcilable enmity and moral warfare between Satan and his followers on the one hand, and the Woman (Mary) and her children on the other hand. God promised to redeem fallen mankind through the Woman and her offspring, (Jesus Christ and the baptized, as adopted children) who would achieve a complete and final victory over Satan and his offspring. Blessed Pope John Paul II wrote:

> "I will put enmity between you and the Woman, and between your offspring and hers; He will strike at your head, while you strike at his heel." (Genesis 3:15).
>
> As we see from the words of the Protogospel, the victory of The Woman's Son will not take place without a hard struggle, a struggle that is to extend through the whole of human history.
>
> The "enmity", foretold at the beginning, is confirmed in the Apocalypse (the book in the Bible of the final events of the Church and the world), in which there recurs the sign of the "Woman", this time "clothed with the sun". (Revelation 12:1).
>
> **Mary, Mother of the Incarnate Word, is placed at the very Center of that enmity, that struggle which accompanies the history of salvation itself.** (Encyclical letter, *Mother of the Redeemer*, Blessed Pope John Paul II, 1987).

The Protogospel is an implicit prophecy of Mary's role as the Immaculate conqueror of Satan (Documents of Vatican II, *Dogmatic Constitution on the Church,* 55) and an explicit prophecy of her role as the Mother of our Redeemer and the Mother of the Church. We see, then, that **Jesus and Mary are the new Adam and Eve whose humility and obedience will defeat the pride and disobedience of Satan by their cooperation in the divine plan of our salvation.** Jesus is our brother, Mary is our mother and we are the adopted children.

> **The Mother of the Redeemer has a precise place in the plan of salvation,** for, "when the time had fully come, God sent forth His Son, born of woman, born under the law, to redeem those who were under the law, so that we might receive adoption as sons, and because you are sons, God has sent the spirit of His Son into our hearts, crying 'Abba! Father!' " (Galatians 4:4-6). (Encyclical Letter, *Mother of the Redeemer,* Blessed Pope John Paul II, 1987, 1).

Mary's Prefigurement in the Old Testament

Mary is prefigured in the Book of Psalms and in the Wisdom books by many passages which refer to her in an implicit manner. The prophecy of the Protogospel also refers to her implicitly. (See Genesis 3:15). The prophecy of Isaiah, however, refers to her explicitly: "Therefore the Lord Himself will give you this sign: the virgin shall be with child, and bear a Son, and shall name Him Immanuel." (Isaiah 7:14). This name means "God is with us" and was fulfilled in Mary's virgin birth of Jesus. (See Matthew 1:23).

As Jesus was prefigured by types in the Old Testament, such as Joseph, so too was Our Lady prefigured by the types of Judith and Esther. (See the Books of Judith and Esther). The stories of these two great women should be read in faith as referring to the triumph of the Immaculate Heart of Mary. Judith cuts off her enemy's head. She is like Mary who strikes Satan's proud head. Esther is a Queen who saves her people from an evil scheme for their destruction. She is like Mary who, ironically, reverses Satan's scheme to destroy her and her children. She delivers them from evil. The praise of Judith is applicable to Mary:

> "You are the glory of Jerusalem, the surpassing joy of Israel; you are the splendid boast of our people. With your own hand you have done all this; You have done good to Israel, and God is pleased with what you have wrought. May you be blessed by the Lord Almighty forever and ever!" And all the people answered, "Amen!" (Judith 15:9, 10).

The Immaculate Conception

The splendid boast of our people (see Judith 15:9) is Mary, the Immaculate Conception, who, because of the great dignity of her role as the Mother of God, was the only creature preserved by God free from every stain of sin, even the original sin, in the first moment of her conception. This great privilege was given to her by God in the consideration of the infinite merits obtained by Jesus. She is *tota pulchra* (all beautiful).

God willed that she be immaculate so that His wondrous plan in the creation of the universe would be reflected in her and Jesus might find in her a worthy gateway through which to come to us. She is the immaculate and virginal shoot from which the divine Flower shall blossom. The doctrine of the Immaculate Conception is implicitly revealed in Sacred Scripture. (See Genesis 3:15; Luke 1:28; Luke 1:41).

This doctrine was infallibly defined by Pope Pius IX in 1854. The charism of infallibility means that there can be no error when the Pope alone as supreme teacher of the faithful, or the Pope and the Bishops, in union with him, agree that a doctrine regarding faith or morals is to be held definitely and absolutely. Pope Pius IX said that the doctrine as follows was revealed by God, and therefore to be believed firmly and constantly by all the faithful: "The Most Holy Virgin Mary was, in the first moment of her conception, by a unique gift of grace and privilege of Almighty God, in view of the merits of Jesus Christ, the Redeemer of mankind, preserved free from all stain of original sin." (Bull *Ineffebilis Deus,* Pope Pius IX, 1854).

As the Immaculate Conception, Mary does not merely have the absence of sin, but the presence of grace. She possesses the fullness of the grace obtained by her Son's redemption. The Eastern Church calls her the "All Holy One."

As such, her life was a pure reflection of the life of God. Her soul was completely filled with grace. Her mind was opened to seek and love the will of God. Her heart was completely filled with love and her body was clothed in the immaculate light of virginal purity. She completely reflected the original plan of the Eternal Father.

As a consequence of her Immaculate Conception, Mary was free from concupiscence (unruly passions) and every personal sin during her entire life. Also, unlike us, she had no moral ignorance, no weakness of the will and no bodily infirmities. She voluntarily incurred sufferings out of her great love.

What Adam and Eve lost by original sin, God renewed in Mary, together with many other gifts which are beyond our comprehension. She is the new Eve, whose virgin birth brought forth Jesus, the new Adam. His obedience made up for the disobedience of Adam and Eve and merited our redemption in Baptism, when we receive the life of grace and become children of God. (See Romans 5:19).

God began His plan to destroy sin and death with the Immaculate Conception. His plan is to clothe us through Mary, in her own immaculateness, and to heal us from sin. Her mission in this plan is to mediate all His graces to us and to fight and defeat the prideful head of Satan who is still at work in the world, prowling like a roaring lion looking for someone to devour. (See 1 Peter 5:8). She is our leader in this battle and applies the graces merited by her Son to us, her children in her army, through our simple faith, trust, humility and obedience. (See Genesis 3:15). **She promised us at Fatima that "in the end my Immaculate Heart will triumph."**

The Annunciation

As a young girl, Mary had prayerfully meditated on the Scriptures. She knew that the Messiah would be born of a Jewish virgin but in her humility she never expected that she would be the Mother of the Redeemer.

The angel Gabriel announced to this teenager that she was chosen to be the Mother of Jesus. Mary responded, "I am the servant of the Lord. Let it be done to me according to thy Word." (Luke 1:38). **With this obedient response to the will of God, Mary contradicted both Satan's disobedience and the disobedience of Adam and Eve.** Mary was the first to accept the Person of Jesus as her Lord and Savior.

The Eternal Word of the Father, the Second Person of the Most Holy Trinity, descended into Mary's pure womb in expectation of her maternal cooperation, to receive from her His human nature and to become, in the flesh, a true man in the divine person of Jesus. This was the Incarnation of Jesus and the beginning of His Redemption, which ended with His Crucifixion.

God established His plan for our salvation in Mary. "This union of the Mother with the Son in the work of salvation was manifested from the time of Christ's virginal conception up to His death." (Documents of Vatican II, *Dogmatic Constitution on the Church*, 57.) Mary was called to be the virgin Mother of our Redeemer and she said "yes!" In her, the divine person and nature of Christ incarnated, shared, redeemed and freed our fallen human nature from sin and death.

"The Word became flesh and made His dwelling among us." (John 1:14). "The Virgin Mary, who at the message of the angel received the Word of God in her heart and her body and gave Life to the world, is acknowledged and honored as being truly the Mother of God and of the Redeemer." (Documents of Vatican II, *Dogmatic Constitution on the Church*, 58).

God could have come into the world as He left it — as an adult on a cloud in the air. He had no need of Mary, but He chose to entrust Himself completely to her as an infant because of her humility and her obedience by which she cooperated in His plan of our salvation. God chose her to reach men. Likewise, we should choose her to reach God by our consecration to her Immaculate Heart.

Mary's role as the Mother of God and of the Redeemer underlies the whole mystery of her identity as the Immaculate Conception and explains everything else about her. However, her role in the divine plan of our salvation continued to manifest itself in union with her Son until His Crucifixion.

The Visitation and Nativity

Mary was inspired by the angel Gabriel's message about her elderly cousin Elizabeth's pregnancy, and in charity she visited her. The Holy Spirit prophesied through Elizabeth, "Blest are you among women and blest is the fruit of your womb." (Luke 1:42). Like Elizabeth, we should say, "But who am I that the mother of my Lord should come to me?" (Luke 1:43).

Mary's Visitation to Elizabeth brought Our Lord to her and her baby, John the Baptist. He was sanctified in his mother's womb, freed from original sin and enriched by grace.

Mary's response in her Magnificat Canticle shows her profound humility by which she gives God all of the glory and acknowledges Him as her Savior. (See Luke 1:46-55). She praises His greatness for pulling down the mighty and exalting the humble.

In this mystery of the Visitation, we see Mary's role in the divine plan of salvation as the instrument of our sanctification. Grace comes to us from Jesus through Mary as the Mediatrix of her Son.

Mary also gave birth to Our Lord for the whole world and brought forth the Light to a world in darkness, which neither expected nor welcomed Him. (See John 1:5). She joyfully showed Him to the shepherds and the Magi. (See Luke 2). The people of Israel awaited this arrival of the Messiah for hundreds of years. Their hope which had been maintained by the voices of the prophets was now rewarded.

In the fullness of time the light of heaven came to a dark, cold cave through Mary. As light passes through a crystal without grazing it, so too did Jesus pass through the veil of Mary's virginal womb preserving her virginity.

In this mystery, Mary foreshadowed in natural life her role in the supernatural life for all time as a bearer of Jesus to unworthy humanity.

The Presentation and the Finding of Jesus in the Temple

Mary and Joseph brought the baby Jesus to the temple in obedience to the law which said that "every first born male shall be consecrated to the Lord." (Luke 2:23).

Mary presented Jesus in the temple and offered Him to the Lord. This was in remembrance of the day in Egypt on which God struck dead the first born of the Egyptians, but spared the Jews.

Simeon received the baby Jesus as the Messiah that was awaited for centuries and as a Savior of all peoples. Simeon prophesied to Mary that "you yourself shall be pierced with a sword...." (Luke 2:35).

This mystery reveals Mary's universal maternal function of bringing Jesus to all peoples. It also reveals that her maternal mission was to be one of profound suffering in an intimate and personal participation in the sorrowful mission of her Son, Jesus.

When Jesus was 12 years old, Mary and Joseph lost Him when they visited Jerusalem. Filled with anguish and sorrow, they searched for Him for three days before finding Him teaching the elders in the temple. (See Luke 2:41-49).

In this mystery, Mary foreshadowed her role of seeking all of her lost children in the supernatural life for all time. In anguish and sorrow, she pities lost sinners and mediates graces for their conversion so that, like Jesus, they may come home with her in obedience and grow in wisdom, age and grace. (See Luke 2:52).

The Crucifixion

Mary stood at the foot of the Cross and mournfully kept her station, with the apostle John, in union with Jesus to the end. (See John 19:25).

Here was fulfilled Simeon's prophecy that a sword of sorrow would pierce her heart. (See Luke 2:35). As the heart of Jesus was pierced by the soldier's lance, so too was the heart of His Mother pierced by this sword of sorrow. (See John 19:34). She voluntarily consented to her suffering and sacrifice, in union with her Son's, but in an unbloody manner.

The soldier's lance released water and blood from the heart of Jesus. (See John 19:34). The water and the blood symbolize the graces of the sacraments of Baptism and the Eucharist, (see 1 John 5:6) by which we are incorporated and nourished in the Church, the Mystical Body of Christ. The sword of sorrow in Mary's heart cooperated in the release of these graces.

> The Council says that this happened "not without a Divine plan" by "suffering deeply with her only-begotten Son and joining herself with her maternal spirit to His Sacrifice, lovingly consenting to the immolation of the Victim to whom she had given birth," in this way Mary "faithfully preserved her union with her Son even to the Cross!" It is a union through faith — the same faith with which she had received the angel's revelation at the Annunciation. (Encyclical Letter, *Mother of the Redeemer*, Blessed Pope John Paul II, 1987, 18, 62).

"Woman, there is your Son." (John 19:26). Jesus identified His Church with John and He identified His Mother with the Woman of Genesis (see Genesis 3:15) and with the Woman of Revelation (see Revelation 12:1).

The expression "Woman" goes to the very heart of the mystery of Mary and indicates the unique role which she has in the divine plan of our salvation. (Encyclical Letter, *Mother of the Redeemer,* Blessed Pope John Paul II, 1987, 24).

Jesus told John, and all of us, "there is your Mother." (John 19:27). **In this mystery, Mary foreshadowed her role as the Mother of the Church.** As Mother of the Church, she is there interceding for us at our Baptism and our Eucharistic receptions. As she was the Mother of the Redeemer in natural life, so is she the Mother of the Church in the supernatural life. (Documents of Vatican II, *Dogmatic Constitution on the Church* 61). St. Louis de Montfort said "God the Son wishes to form Himself and so to speak, to incarnate Himself in His members every day by His dear Mother . . . ." (*True Devotion to Mary,* St. Louis de Montfort, 31). She cooperates in giving birth to us in the supernatural life and in sustaining us in it by the graces obtained through her maternal intercession. Mary's motherhood in the supernatural life will last without interruption until the eternal fulfillment of all the elect. (Documents of Vatican II, *Dogmatic Constitution on the Church,* 62).

Pentecost

After the Ascension of Jesus into heaven, the Apostles stayed in the upper room in Jerusalem, where they devoted themselves to constant prayer. Mary was with them. (See Acts 1:1-4). As a result of this constant prayer, the Holy Spirit descended upon them on the day of Pentecost. (See Acts 2:1-4).

As the Holy Spirit had overshadowed Mary at the Annunciation (see Luke 1:35), He descended, by her intercession, on her and the Apostles at Pentecost.

In this mystery Mary foreshadowed her role of bringing us the Holy Spirit, our Sanctifier, whose fruits and gifts we receive by the merits obtained by Jesus Christ through her intercession. The Holy Spirit constantly brings faith to completion by His gifts. His pathway is the Immaculate Heart of Mary through which He passes to us.

As Mary brought forth Jesus in natural life, so she now brings Him forth in the supernatural life in the Church by her spouse, the Holy Spirit.

> And so, in the redemptive economy of grace, brought about through the action of the Holy Spirit, there is a unique correspondence between the moment of the Incarnation of the Word and the moment of the birth of the Church. The person who links these two moments is Mary: Mary at Nazareth and Mary in the Upper Room at Jerusalem. In both cases her discreet yet

essential presence indicates the path of birth from the Holy Spirit! Thus she who is present in the mystery of Christ as Mother becomes — by the will of the Son and the power of the Holy Spirit — present in the mystery of the Church. In the Church too she continues to be a maternal presence, as is shown by the words spoken from the Cross: "Woman, behold your Son! Behold your Mother." (Encyclical Letter, *Mother of the Redeemer,* Blessed Pope John Paul II, 1987, 24).

The Assumption and Coronation

Mary's place is now at the right hand of her Son enjoying the fullness of His joys and delights after her Assumption into heaven and Coronation by Him as Queen of the Universe. (Documents of Vatican II, *Dogmatic Constitution on the Church,* 59). She is Queen both by her perfection and by her power, given to her by the Son, "of bestowing upon us the fruits of the redemption." (Encyclical Letter, *Ad Coeli Reginam,* Pope Pius XII, 1954).

Jesus had not suffered His "faithful one to undergo corruption" (see Psalm 16:10), but had assumed her body and soul into the glory of heaven at the end of her earthly life.

This doctrine was infallibly declared by Pope Pius XII, on November 1, 1950, as follows: "By the authority of our Lord Jesus Christ, of the blessed Apostles Peter and Paul, and by Our own authority, We pronounce, declare, and define it to be a divinely revealed dogma; that the Immaculate Mother of God, Mary, ever Virgin, after her life on earth, was assumed, body and soul, into heavenly glory." (Constitution, *Munificentissimus Deus,* Pope Pius XII, III, 44).

This doctrine is implicitly, although obscurely, revealed in Sacred Scripture (see Genesis 3:15; Psalm 16:10-11; Psalm 132:8; Revelation 11:19) as well as in Tradition. However, the living Teaching Authority of the Church, whose Spirit of truth is with her at all times, can infallibly discern and declare what has been divinely revealed, regardless of how cryptic the revelation may be.

As Mary had shared in Christ's struggle against Satan and in His victory over sin on Calvary and His victory over death by His Resurrection and Ascension, so now she, as the New Eve, shares the fruit of these victories by her Assumption. (See Pope Pius XII, *Acta Apostolicae Sedis* 42:768). On earth Mary always associated with her Son through her role as mother. Now in heaven she is associated in His glory, having a glorified body like His own with which she still loves us as our mother through her Immaculate Heart.

In this mystery, Mary's role in the divine plan of our salvation is culminated. As death is the consequence of original sin, her Assumption is the consequence of her Immaculate Conception. Jesus shared with His mother His triumph over sin and death and assumed, glorified and coronated her body and soul. She was "exalted by the Lord as Queen over all things. . . . " (Documents of Vatican II, *Dogmatic Constitution on the Church*, 59). Her Queenship rests on her divine motherhood. She is the mother of Jesus, who "will rule over the house of Jacob forever and His reign will be without end." (Luke 1:32). However, she "is to be called Queen because she, by the will of God, had an outstanding part in the work of our eternal salvation." (Encyclical Letter, *Ad Coeli Reginam*, Pope Pius XI, 1954).

Mary now stands at His right hand, interceding, mediating and dispensing to us all of the graces that His redemption merited. "Taken up to heaven, she did not lay aside this saving role, but by her manifold acts of intercession continues to win for us gifts of eternal salvation." (Documents of Vatican II, *Dogmatic Constitution on the Church*, 62). In this role, she will lead us to the ultimate defeat of Satan and his followers through the victory of her Immaculate Heart in the world.

Co-Redemptrix

Our redemption was merited solely by the passion and death of Our Lord and Savior, Jesus Christ. (See Hebrews 9:15; 1 Timothy 2:5). By His redemption He paid the full price to satisfy God's justice and to buy us back from the consequences of sin, death and the loss of heaven caused by the original sin of Adam and Eve. By His redemption, He merited for all humanity the supernatural life of grace and our salvation and the glory of heaven. This is the *objective* redemption.

However, these graces must be applied to us through our following in Christ's footsteps on our earthly pilgrimage. Jesus said that "if a man wishes to come after me, he must deny his very self, take up his cross, and begin to follow in my footsteps." (Matthew 16:24). As the Cyrenean helped Jesus to carry His Cross, so we must join our efforts to His and participate in His redemptive work.

This is the *subjective* redemption by which, according to Christ's will, all members of the Church, His Mystical Body, follow His footsteps in cooperation with His redemptive work, so that the graces merited by Him may be applied to His greater glory. This is what Saint Paul meant when he said that "in my own flesh I fill up what is lacking in the sufferings of Christ for the sake of His body, the Church." (Colossians 1:24).

Jesus is the only Redeemer because He alone is the mediator between God and men. However, He has willed to take into partnership in His redemptive work all of those whom He redeemed in order that the merciful work of His love may shine forth through us.

This merciful work of love is shared by all of us who unite our sufferings with Christ and thereby "fill up what is lacking in the sufferings of Christ. ..." (Colossians 1:24).

Mary encouraged this merciful work of love at Fatima when she said, "Pray, pray very much, and make sacrifices for sinners; for many souls go to hell, because there are none to sacrifice themselves and to pray for them." (*Fatima in Lucia's Own Words,* Cambridge MA 02138: The Ravengate Press, 1976, p. 171).

Mary followed in her Son's footsteps and cooperated in the objective redemption (Documents of Vatican II, *Dogmatic Constitution on the Church,* 58) and still cooperates in the subjective redemption. Therefore she can be called our Co-Redemptrix. Her role is as perfect leader and Mediatrix in the subjective redemption of humanity, applying the graces merited by her Son, with her cooperation, in the accomplished objective redemption.

Pope Benedict XV wrote in *Inter Sodalicia* (1918):

> With her suffering and dying Son, Mary endured suffering and almost death. She gave up her mother's rights over her Son to procure the salvation of mankind, and to appease the divine justice, she, as much as she could, immolated her Son, so that one can truly affirm that together with Christ she has redeemed the human race.

As the Fall of man came about through the cooperation of Adam and Eve in the original sin, so did the restoration of man come about through the cooperation of Jesus and Mary in the Redemption.

Mediatrix of All Graces

Mary is the Mediatrix of All Graces. Blessed Pope John Paul II said, "This role of Mary, totally grounded in that of Christ and radically subordinated to it, in no way obscures or diminishes the unique mediation of Christ, but rather shows its power." (Blessed Pope John Paul II, Apostolic Letter, *The Rosary of the Virgin Mary,* 2002, 1:15).

The sole mediator between God and humanity is Jesus Christ, who gave Himself as a ransom for all. (See 1 Timothy 2:5-6). A mediator is a friendly third party who interposes between parties who are not united. Jesus is our mediator with God because He shared our human nature so that we could share His divine nature through the graces merited by His passion and death.

Such mediation does not exclude a subordinate mediation by Mary between Jesus and us through her intercession and dispensation of the graces merited by Him. It is in this sense that Vatican Council II probably used the title "Mediatrix." (Documents of Vatican II, *Dogmatic Constitution on the Church,* 62). However, neither this title nor that of "Co-Redemptrix" has been solemnly dogmatically defined. Nevertheless, "all theologians now agree in holding this most tender and salutary doctrine that Mary is the Mediatrix of all graces." (Decree of the Congregation of Rites approved by Pope Pius XII, January 11, 1942, [*Acta Apostolicae Sedis*] 34:44). As Jesus is our mediator with God the Father of our redemption, Mary is our Mediatrix with God the Son of His graces.

It is the will of God to exercise the power of Christ's mediation by the application of His merited graces to us through His mother, our Mediatrix in the subjective redemption. (Documents of Vatican II, *Dogmatic Constitution on the Church,* 60). Jesus is the source of Mary's mediation which makes available to us the richness of His mediation through her Immaculate Heart and the ministry of priests.

As Mary was our Co-Redemptrix while still on her earthly pilgrimage and gave us Jesus, the source of all graces, so now is she our Mediatrix in heaven who distributes those graces to us. As mother of the source of all graces, can she not be the mother of all graces from the source?

The title of Mediatrix befits Mary's dignity because she did such great things for our salvation as a participant with her Son in His objective redemption. She furnished Him with a body with which she suffered in His passion. Jesus makes her a continuing participant in the subjective redemption by placing her in charge of His merits to be distributed by her to the redeemed. In this way, she frees sinners, enriches the needy, elevates the just and affords a universal refuge to all men.

Mary has demonstrated this role as Mediatrix very tenderly as a Mother, particularly at Medjugorje. There she has diffused graces which have converted sinners, healed the sick and attracted millions to her as their refuge.

Pope Leo XIII quotes St. Bernardine of Siena as saying: "Every grace . . . has a threefold course. For, in accord with excellent order, it is dispensed from God to Christ, from Christ to the Virgin, and from the Virgin to us." (Pope Leo XIII, September 22, 1891. [*Acta Apostolicae Sedis*] 24:195-196).

St. Louis de Montfort says, "To go to Jesus, we must go to Mary; she is our mediatrix of intercession. To go to God the Father, we must go to Jesus; for He is our mediator of redemption." (*True Devotion to Mary,* St. Louis de Montfort, 86).

As Jesus is the head of His Mystical Body, she is the heart and all of the graces flow from the head through the heart to us as all of the other members of His Mystical Body. This is simply the will of God, which was decreed by Jesus on the Cross and carried out at Mary's Coronation. It was then that all of the graces which flow from the Father, merited for us by the Son and given by the Holy Spirit, were deposited with Mary as the treasurer for her distribution to the world according to her intercessory will, which is one with God's. (*Mediator Dei,* Pope Pius XII, 1947). As the Father gave all to the Son (see John 3:35), so did the Son give all graces to His mother for us.

The mediation of the Immaculate Heart of Mary is two-way. She mediates all graces to us from God and she also mediates to God from us all of our prayers, sacrifices and good works, embellishing them with her own merits. She mediates the gratitude which we owe to God by which He is glorified.

Mary's role as Mediatrix was foreshadowed at the wedding feast of Cana, where she interceded with Jesus and mediated His gift of new wine. (See John 2). Similarly, Mary, as Mother of the Church, obtains the spiritual nourishment of all graces necessary for our eternal salvation. (Encyclical Letter, *Mother of the Redeemer,* Blessed Pope John Paul, II, 1987. 21.7). The mystery of her mystical maternity, first foreshadowed at the Annunciation, then at Cana and finally at the Crucifixion, is now carried out in her role as Mediatrix.

At Medjugorje, on August 25, 1987, Mary said, *"Dear children,* **seek from God the graces which He is giving you through me.** *I am ready to intercede with God for all that you seek so your holiness may be complete. Therefore, dear children, do not forget to seek, because God has permitted me to obtain graces for you."*

As Queen of the Universe, Mary will exercise her role as Universal Mediatrix of all graces "until the eternal fulfillment of the elect." (Documents of Vatican II, *Dogmatic Constitution on the Church,* 62), when the work of the redemption is completed and Jesus will subject Himself and all created things to the Father, that God may be all in all. (See 1 Corinthians 15:27-28).

The Virtues of Mary

In her lifetime, Mary practiced all virtues to perfection. "However, Mary is not unapproachable to us because of her sublime privileges and virtues. She journeyed, as we do, in faith through the joys, sufferings and trials of everyday life. The faithful still strive to conquer sin and increase in holiness. And so they turn their eyes to Mary who shines forth to the whole community of the elect as the model of virtues." (Documents of Vatican II, *Dogmatic Constitution on the Church*, 65).

We have in Mary no other person more approachable, more simple and more human. Mary is our model in the pilgrimage of faith. She is an attractive model since she practiced the virtues in ordinary, everyday life, like most of us, by fulfilling lowly daily duties and leading a hidden, retired life in joy and in sorrow.

She practiced obedient faith by believing the message of the angel Gabriel that she would be the Mother of God. She practiced ardent charity by visiting and caring for her elderly pregnant cousin, Elizabeth. In maternal love she gave birth to her Son. In obedience to the Law she presented Him in the temple. She docilely accepted God's will by receiving Simeon's prophecy of her suffering and by accepting her Son's mission to do the work of His Father.

A brief review of her pilgrimage of faith through the mysteries of her life exemplifies her practice of the virtues and should move us to imitate them. She practiced lively faith and the docile acceptance of the Word of God (see Luke 1:26-38, 1:45, 11:27-28; John 2:5); generous obedience (see Luke 1:38); genuine humility (see Luke 1:48); solicitous charity (see Luke 1:39-56); profound wisdom (see Luke 1:29, 34; 2:19; 33:51); worship of God manifested in the fulfillment of religious duties (see Luke 2:21-41); in gratitude for gifts received (see Luke 1:46-49); in her offering in the Temple (see Luke 2:22-24) and in her prayer in the midst of the Apostles (see Acts 1:12-14).

She practiced fortitude in exile (see Matthew 2:13-23) and in suffering (see Luke 2:34-35, 49; John 19:25); poverty reflecting dignity and trust in God (see Luke 1:48, 2:24); attentive care for her Son, from His humble birth to the ignominy of the Cross (see Luke 2:1-11); virginal purity (see Matthew 1:18-25; Luke 1:26-38); and strong and chaste married love.

St. Louis de Montfort lists the ten principal virtues of Mary: her profound humility; her lively faith; her blind obedience; her continual prayer; her universal mortification; her divine purity; her ardent charity; her heroic patience; her angelic sweetness and her divine wisdom. (*True Devotion to Mary*, St. Louis de Montfort, 108). These virtues will be ours if we study and follow her example. St. Louis tells us:

> The predestinate keep the way of our Blessed Lady; their good mother; that is to say, they imitate her. It is on this point that they are truly happy and truly devout, and bear the infallible mark of their predestination, according to the words this good mother speaks to them: Blessed are they who practice my virtues (Proverbs 8:32), and with the help of divine grace walk in the footsteps of my life. During

life they are happy in this world through the abundance of grace and sweetness which I impart to them from my fullness, and more abundantly to them than to others who do not imitate me so closely. They are happy in their death, at which I am ordinarily present myself, that I may conduct them to the joys of eternity; for never has any one of my good servants been lost who imitated my virtues during life. (*True Devotion to Mary*, St. Louis de Montfort, 200).

The Divine Mary

During the Liturgy of the Eucharist, when the priest pours wine and water into the chalice, he says, "By the mystery of this water and wine may we come to share in the divinity of Christ who humbled Himself to share in our humanity."

As Christ shared in our humanity, so too, by grace, do we share in His divinity. A soul in the state of grace is divinized. That is, it shares the very divine nature of God. (See 2 Peter 1:4). Mary shares in the divine nature to the highest degree.

"All glorious is the king's daughter as she enters; her raiment is threaded with spun gold." (Psalm 45:14). As the daughter of an earthly king partakes of his royalty, so too does Mary, the daughter of Our Father, the heavenly King, partake of His divinity.

"Consequently, through the power of the Holy Spirit, in the order of grace, which is a participation in the divine nature, Mary receives life from Him to whom she herself, in the order of earthly generation, gave life as a mother." (Encyclical Letter, *Mother of the Redeemer*, Blessed Pope John Paul, II, 1987, 10).

So it is that St. Louis calls her "the divine Mary." (*True Devotion to Mary*, St. Louis de Montfort, 6, 217). By this he meant that she is so transformed into Christ by grace, that she lives no more, and is as though she were not, Christ living and reigning in her more perfectly than in all the angels and the blessed. (*True Devotion to Mary*, St. Louis de Montfort, 63).

Likewise, St. Maximilian Kolbe stated that Mary was "the creature most elevated among creatures, the most perfect creature, divine." (Conference July 26, 1939 as quoted in Piacentini, Ernest, *The Immaculate Conception*, Kenosha, Wisconsin: Franciscan Marytown Press, 1975, p. 164).

Mary's human nature was overshadowed by the divine nature at the Annunciation. (See Luke 1:35). She continued to merit grace through her earthly pilgrimage, so that her human nature could be said to have been completely divinized by grace, because of her cooperation in the objective and subjective redemptions.

4: Warnings, Chastisements and the New Era of Peace

Our Lady of Fatima prophesied an Era of Peace and Blessed Pope John Paul II announced a New Era of Peace. However, these eras will not come without warnings and chastisements.

A "warning" is a call to change, to conversion and repentance, or to suffer from a chastisement or punishment. Mary's ten secrets at Medjugorje contain both warnings and chastisements.

The prophets warned us to stop sinning or be punished. God never inflicts chastisements without warning us through His servants, the prophets. God's love for His sinful children is shown through the prophets, who issue warnings to turn back to God with faith and to pray and fast, or to suffer chastisements.

Warnings and Chastisements

Jesus gave the same warning that the prophet John the Baptist gave. They both gave the same call, "Repent, for the kingdom of heaven is at hand." (Matthew 3:2; 4:17). After the Tower of Siloam fell and killed eighteen people, Jesus was asked if they were guiltier than all of the others in Jerusalem. He replied, in a statement that still applies today, "Certainly not! But I tell you, unless you repent, you will all perish as they did." (Luke 13:5).

A chastisement is a punishment sent by God, or by others and allowed by God, in order to help sinners to convert. There are many examples of chastisements in the Bible: the Great Flood (Genesis 6:5); the destruction of Sodom and Gomorrah (Genesis 28:20); the earthquake that swallowed up Korah and his followers (Numbers 16:32) and the plagues of Egypt (Exodus 6:6; 12:12).

King David sinned grievously by counting the number of his army, rather than trusting in the strength of God. He was punished and God sent a pestilence that killed 70,000 people. (2 Samuel 24:15). Later God allowed the Babylonian Captivity and the destruction of Jerusalem.

The prophets warned of biblical chastisements. Isaiah, Jeremiah, Ezekiel and Jesus all prophesied the destruction of Jerusalem for its sins. (See Isaiah 1; Jeremiah 1; Ezekiel 23; Luke 21:5-6; 20-24). These were prophecies of divine chastisements that were fulfilled. Jesus' prophecy of the destruction of Jerusalem was fulfilled with the killings of tens of thousands by the Roman General Titus in the year 70 A. D. (See Luke 19:41-44; 21:5-6; 20-24).

God's purpose for chastisements is medicinal. God wants to bring humanity to repentance and conversion and to live in His love and grace. Scripture says that God chastises those He loves. "Whoever is dear to me I reprove and chastise. Be earnest about it, therefore. Repent!" (Revelation 3:19).

The Letter to the Hebrews says that chastisements are to make the righteous holy, just as an earthly father disciplines his children to teach them to be good. (See Hebrews 12:5-13).

God does judge. Hell is eternal punishment for unrepented sin. It is a real consequence to wrongdoing and deservedly suffered. But to save us from hell, God chooses to impose chastisements. These are intended to discourage us from self-injury and to encourage us to rectify our lives. Sin is separation from God and violation of His loving plan. Punishment shows sinners what they are doing to themselves. So God permits humankind to experience the consequences of sin.

God's chastisements are not for destruction, but for *reconstruction* — to bring us to repentance and conversion and back to Him and to His divine mercy through the forgiveness of our sins. Divine judgments are not to consume us, but to purify us. They are not to condemn us, but to redeem us. They are not an end, but a chance for a new beginning. We can bring about this new beginning through prayer, fasting and the sacraments of Confession and Eucharist.

God creates everything good. Evil comes from creatures' abuses of their freedom, and punishment for sin is not arbitrarily imposed by God.

Human punishment often has the character of a more or less vengeful reaction, but God's punishment has nothing of this character. It comes from His love and desire to save us.

Without excluding created freedom, God "desires all men to be saved and to come to the knowledge of the truth." (1 Timothy 2-4). Jesus comes to save, not to condemn. (See John 3:17; 12:7).

God's justice ultimately consists in being faithful to His gifts of life and freedom. God simply cannot be unfaithful. (See 2 Timothy 2:12-13). God tries every means to win the love of sinners who initially reject Him, but still might repent. In the death of our Lord Jesus, we see how far He goes. "God so loved the world that He gave His only Son." (John 3:16). In the Letter to the Hebrews, it says, "My son, do not regard lightly the discipline of the Lord, nor lose courage when you are punished by Him. For the Lord disciplines him whom He loves, and chastises every son whom He receives."

(Hebrews 12:5-6). The innocent also suffer from chastisements, as shown by the trials of Job.

Chastisements of the Innocent

God allowed the chastisements of the innocent Job for His greater glory. Job's story is told in the Book of Job. He was an innocent man who was "blameless and upright who feared God and avoided evil." (Job 1:1). He had many children, animals and much property and was "greater than any of the men of the East." (Job 1:3). God allowed that he suffer chastisements and lose it all.

The Book of Job shows that God allowed him to be chastised through Satan by means that still happen today: enemy raiders (like today's terrorists); forces of nature, such as lightning and great wind (like today's hurricanes and tornados); a loathsome disease causing boils and scabs (like today's AIDS); and the death and loss of property, animals, employees and children.

Job is a model of a good attitude towards the chastisements of innocent people. He was humble and realized that God allows the chastisements of innocent people like himself. He recognized that God does not have to justify His actions to men, that He is almighty and omnipotent and that one must humbly accept suffering and trust in God, that "all things work for good for those who love God." (Romans 8:28).

We should say with Job, "Happy is the man whom God reproves! The Almighty's chastening do not reject. For He wounds, but He binds up; He smites, but His hands give healing." (Job 5:17-18).

We should imitate him and his acceptance of chastisements. Job said, "Naked I came forth from my mother's womb, and naked shall I go back again. The Lord gave and the Lord has taken away; blessed be the name of the Lord!" (Job 1:21) "We accept good things from God; and should we not accept evil?" (Job 2:10).

Finally, we should stop questioning God and trust in His ways of Divine Providence. Job said, "I know that you can do all things and that no purpose of yours can be hindered. I have dealt with great things that I do not understand; things too wonderful for me, which I cannot know. I had heard of you by word of mouth, but now my eye has seen you. Therefore, I disown what I have said, and repent in dust and ashes." (Job 42:2-6).

Jesus Christ was the totally innocent one that suffered from chastisement. The prophet Isaiah prophesied, "But He was wounded for our transgressions, He was bruised for our iniquities; upon Him was the chastisement that made us whole, and with His stripes we were healed. . . . But the Lord laid upon Him the guilt of us all." (Isaiah 53:5-6).

Chastisements and God's Love

God's chastisements can be brought to us through Himself directly (such as the destruction of Sodom and Gomorrah), through nature (such as the Great Flood), or through the evil hands of others (such as the Romans' destruction of Jerusalem), resulting in the death of innocent people. Jesus Himself is the prime example. God allows this for a greater good. God's chastisements bring suffering which is mysteriously meritorious to those who accept it, abandon themselves and offer it to Him. Suffering brings us to repentance that brings God's merciful forgiveness, healing and union with Him.

God really loves us, even if He allows the innocent to suffer chastisements. The Bible assures us of God's love. St. John the Evangelist wrote, "For God so loved the world that He gave His only Son, that whoever believes in Him should not perish but have eternal life. For God sent the Son into the world, not to condemn the world, but that the world might be saved through Him." (John 3:16-17).

God passed before Moses and proclaimed, "The Lord, the Lord, a merciful and gracious God, slow to anger and rich in kindness and fidelity, continuing his kindness for a thousand generations, and forgiving wickedness and crime and sin; yet not declaring the guilty guiltless, but punishing children and grandchildren to the third and fourth generation for their fathers' wickedness!" (Exodus 34:6-7). However, fear of chastisements is useless, what is needed is trust.

"We should have confidence on the day of judgment. . . ." (1 John 4:17). "Be sincere of heart, be steadfast, and do not be alarmed when disaster comes. Trust Him and He will uphold you, follow a straight path and hope in Him." (Sirach 2:2-6).

St. John wrote, "So we know and believe the love God has for us. God is love, and he who abides in love abides in God, and God abides in him. In this is love perfected with us, that we may have confidence for the day of judgment, because as He is so are we in this world. There is no fear in love, but perfect love casts out fear. For fear has to do with punishment, and he who fears is not perfected in love." (1 John 9-10. 16-18).

Mary, Prophetess of Chastisements

We are living in an era of moral darkness and a Culture of Death. Atheism, paganism, rejection of Church teachings, sexual perversion, infidelity, corruptions and abortions are rampant throughout the world. These sins of humanity cry out to God for vengeance and His chastisement.

God's chastisements are His secrets which He reveals to His prophets. They speak His word and reveal them to us so that by repentance and conversion we can mitigate or avoid them. "For the Lord God does nothing without revealing His secrets to His servants, the prophets." (Amos 3:7).

God revealed chastisements to His prophets, so that those whom they warned could mitigate or avoid them. He revealed to Noah the Great Flood; to Abraham and Lot the destruction of Sodom and Gomorrah; to Joseph the seven years' famine in Egypt; to Moses the plagues of Egypt; and to Jonah the destruction of Nineveh. These were prophets sent by God in the Old Testament. In modern times, He has sent His mother as the prophetess of chastisements.

As the prophetess of chastisements, Mary has warned the world in modern times to repent and convert or suffer chastisements, long before her apparitions at Medjugorje. In 1917, at Fatima, Portugal during World War I, she prophesied destruction as a divine chastisement and punishment for sins. She said, *"**War is a punishment for sins**"* and that God was *"about to punish the world for its crimes by means of war, famine and persecutions of the Church and of the Holy Father."* She also warned that if her messages were not obeyed, *"nations will be annihilated."*

On July 13, 1917, she revealed the vision of the Third Secret of Fatima. Pope Emeritus Benedict XVI, then Cardinal Joseph Ratzinger, interpreted this vision and said, "**This represents the threat of judgment [chastisements] which looms over the world.** Today the prospect that the world might be reduced to ashes by a sea of fire [as Mary prophesied at Akita, Japan in 1973] no longer seems pure fantasy: man himself, with his inventions, has forged the flaming sword. The vision then shows the power which stands opposed to the force of destruction — the splendor of the Mother of God and . . . the summons to penance. . . . The vision speaks of dangers and how we might be saved from them."

We have been saved from these dangers or they have been mitigated by Mary's intercession. However, the threat of judgment still looms over the world. Mary is the prophetess of coming chastisements. She comes in love for all of her earthly children to warn us, so that we might be able to do something about it.

On October 13, 1973, at Akita, Japan, Mary said, *"**If men do not repent and better themselves, the Father will inflict a terrible punishment on all humanity. It will be a punishment greater than the deluge, such as one will never have seen before.** Fire will fall from the sky and will wipe out a great part of humanity, the good as well as the bad, sparing neither priests nor faithful. The survivors will find themselves so desolate that they will envy the dead."*

In 1981, at Kibeho, Mary said, "*I am concerned with and turning to the whole world to repent because otherwise* **the world is on the edge of catastrophe**."

In 1983, at Medjugorje, Mirjana told Fr. Vlasic that the chastisement of **the tenth secret is "totally bad and cannot be lessened whatsoever."**

Mary still appears throughout the world pleading for prayer and fasting to bring conversions and peace. The alternative, she warns, is to suffer chastisements.

She warned Father Gobbi of the Marian Movement of Priests while he was in the United States on November 15, 1990, "*Abortions – these killings of innocent children, that cry for vengeance before the face of God – have spread and are performed in every part of your homeland. The moment of divine justice and of great mercy has now arrived!* **You will know the hour of weakness and poverty, the hour of suffering and defeat, the purifying hour of the great chastisement**."

As these calamities approach, we should prepare for them and protect ourselves against them. Jesus told us to "be prepared." He said:

> For as it was in the days of Noah, so it will be at the coming of the Son of Man. In those days before the flood, they were eating and drinking, marrying and giving in marriage, up to the day that Noah entered the ark.
>
> They did not know until the flood came and carried them all away. So will it also be at the coming of the Son of Man.
>
> Two men will be out in the field; one will be taken, and one will be left. Two women will be grinding at the mill; one will be taken, and one will be left. Therefore, **stay awake! For you do not know on which day your Lord will come**. Be sure of this: if the master of the house had known the hour of night when the thief was coming, he would have stayed awake and not let his house be broken into. So too, you also must be prepared, for at an hour you do not expect, the Son of Man will come. (Matthew 24:37-44).

Protection from Chastisements

Chastisements can be averted (turned away or avoided) or mitigated (lessened in severity), if people respond to the warning. For example, the prophet Jonah warned Nineveh (ancient Iraq) that it would be destroyed in forty days. But the people repented, prayed and fasted and the chastisement was averted. (See Jonah 3).

History shows that heeding the call to repentance is critical. At the preaching of Jonah, Nineveh repented and was spared its chastisement. At the preaching of Jesus, Jerusalem did not repent and was chastised by its utter destruction by the Romans.

Mary told Sr. Agnes of Akita, "*Pray very much the prayers of the Rosary.* ***I alone am able still to save you from the calamities which approach.*** *Those who place their confidence in me will be saved.*"

At Medjugorje, Mirjana said that the tenth secret chastisement is "unconditional." However, chastisements can be mitigated by prayer and penance. According to visionary Mirjana we are close to chastisement and so she says to "convert yourselves as quickly as possible. Open your hearts to God."

Our attitude towards chastisements should be as Mary told Jelena, another visionary at Medjugorje, "*Don't think about wars, chastisements, evil. It is when you concentrate on these things that you are on the way to enter into them. Your responsibility is to accept divine peace, to live it.*"

Excessive curiosity regarding the prophesied chastisements should be replaced by confidence and obedience to Mary's requests for conversion, faith, prayer, fasting and consecration to her Immaculate Heart.

God recently gave us other means of protection through the devotions to Jesus King of All Nations and Our Lady of America. The Jesus, King of All Nations, Devotion contains prayers and promises for protection against chastisements.(See Appendix A). The promises to those who embrace the Devotion include protection from harm and mitigation of chastisements and all forms of God's justice. The Devotion is consistent with Scripture, Tradition and the Teaching Authority of the Church. It was granted the *Nihil Obstat,* which is a declaration that the devotion is free of doctrinal and moral error.

To mitigate (lessen) chastisements and to help us save souls, Jesus asked us to pray the Novena in Honor of Jesus as True King and made us a promise. He asked us to pray, "*Forgive us, O Sovereign King, our sins against you. Jesus, you are a King of Mercy. We have deserved your Just Judgment. Have mercy on us, Lord, and forgive us. We trust in your Great Mercy! O most awe inspiring King, we bow before you and pray; May your Reign, your Kingdom, be recognized on earth!*" (*Journal* 29). He promised us, "**Each time you say these prayers, I will mitigate the severity of the chastisements upon your country.**" (*Journal* 41).

Jesus also revealed His only medal in the world and promised us protection if we wore it. Our Lady of America also revealed a medal and promised us protection against evil spirits. (See Chapter 5 for an explanation of these medals.)

In His will, **God can rescue the devout from chastisements**. St. Peter writes, "For if God did not spare the angels when they sinned, but condemned them to the chains of Tartarus and handed them over to be kept for judgment; and if He did not spare the ancient world, even though He preserved Noah, a herald of righteousness, together with seven others, when He brought a flood upon the godless world; and if He condemned the cities of Sodom and Gomorrah to destruction, reducing them to ashes, making them an example for the godless people of what is coming; and if He rescued Lot, a righteous man oppressed by the licentious conduct of unprincipaled people, then the Lord knows how to rescue the devout from trial and to keep the unrighteous under punishment for the day of judgment...." (2 Peter 2:4-9).

Hope for the World

Through the prophet Jeremiah, God announced, "I know well the plans I have in mind for you, says the Lord, for your welfare, not for woe! **Plans to give you a future full of hope**." (Jeremiah 29:11). According to St. Paul, "Hope will not leave us disappointed, because the love of God has been poured out in our hearts through the Holy Spirit who has been given to us." (Romans 5:5).

"Hope is the confident expectation of divine blessing." (*CCC* 2290). I asked Mirjana if she had this same confidence that we will receive God's blessing. She said, "Yes, yes, because God is my Father and He loves us and He sends His mother for so many years here to Medjugorje to help us to find Jesus, to find a good way, where we will meet Jesus and have real peace. Look at me. I am always joking, smiling, living my life with God and Blessed Mary with hope, because my faith is hope. I hope in God's love. I hope that He will judge me with love, I don't think about secrets."

Pope Emeritus Benedict XVI, then Cardinal Ratzinger, wrote, "The vision of the third part of the 'secret' [of Fatima], so distressing at first, concludes with an image of hope: no suffering is in vain, and it is a suffering Church, a Church of martyrs, which becomes a sign-post for man in his search for God."

Blessed Pope John Paul II recognized signs of hope for the world. He said, "With full confidence let us place under the vigilant intercession of Holy Mary... the prospect of the Third Millennium. The Third Millennium remains for us a horizon of very stimulating reflections, because it makes us look forward in hope. The Blessed Mary is the guide in the new exodus towards the future."

In his Apostolic Letter, *On the Coming of the Third Millennium*, he said, **"Only God knows what the future holds. But we are certain that He is the Lord of history and directs it to His own end with our cooperation in hope. It will be the fulfillment of a divine plan of love for all humanity and for each one of us. That is why as we look into the future, we are full** of hope and are not overcome with fear. The journey . . . is a great journey of hope."

The Pope also said, "As the third millennium of the redemption draws near, God is preparing a great springtime for Christianity, and we can already see its first signs . . . . Christian hope sustains us in committing ourselves fully to the New Evangelization and to the worldwide mission, and leads us to pray as Jesus taught us: 'Thy will be done, on earth as it is in heaven.' (Matthew 6:10)." (Blessed Pope John Paul II, Encyclical Letter, *Mission of the Redeemer* 86).

In his Apostolic Letter, *On the Coming of the Third Millennium,* the Holy Father closed his remarks and said, "**Christians are called to prepare . . . by renewing their hope** in the definitive coming of the kingdom of God, preparing for it daily in their hearts in the Christian community to which they belong, in their particular social context, and in the world history itself."

The Triumph of the Immaculate Heart of Mary

As Jesus is the head of the Mystical Body of Christ, the Church, so Mary is its heart and we are its humble feet walking our pilgrimage in faith directed by the head through the heart. This heart is like a prism diffusing all graces from the pure light of the holy Trinity in all its varied colors to us. It is the gate of heaven through which passes the love of God to renew the whole world.

The word "heart" as used in Scripture often means the higher part of the soul, the interior perfections. With reference to Mary it refers to her Immaculate Conception, fullness of grace and blessedness. (See Luke 1:28, 42).

Mary's Immaculate Heart exists in her glorified body which still loves and suffers for all humanity. Mary's heart is immaculate because it is without sin, as a consequence of the Immaculate Conception. It is the center of her ever-virgin being which perfectly loves God and us. As she is united with the Sacred Heart of Jesus so too is she united with our hearts and our lives, joys and sorrows.

Her Immaculate Heart also symbolizes her interior life (see Luke 2:19, 51), where she reflected her joys and sorrows, her virtues and hidden perfections, her virginal love for God and her maternal love for Jesus and all humanity.

Her heart is also the heart of a mother, a real living motherly heart which watches over us, hears our cries and helps us by her tender care for us.

She knows at every moment everything that concerns us — our fears, anxieties, faults, temptations and sins. As our spiritual mother her

Immaculate Heart mediates our prayers to God and dispenses God's graces to us.

As a mirror, her heart reflects the most pure light of the Trinity where the Father finds His design intact and perfectly realized from which He receives His greatest Glory from a creature.

The centrality of her being is symbolized by her physical heart as the seat of her love and her spiritual heart as the seat of her interior perfections and her entire interior affective and moral life.

Mary revealed at Fatima that Jesus wants to establish in the world devotion to her Immaculate Heart. If we truly love Our Lady we should heed her request and consecrate ourselves to her Immaculate Heart. Jacinta, another Fatima visionary, said that God has entrusted peace to the Immaculate Heart of Mary. Mary, in turn, told Sister Lucia that she would be her refuge and the way that would lead her to God.

At Fatima, Mary said, "In the end, my Immaculate Heart will triumph." Blessed Pope John Paul II believed that the Medjugorje apparitions were a continuation and fulfillment of the apparitions at Fatima. Mirjana said on October 3, 2009, that Mary told her, "*What I started in Fatima, I will finish in Medjugorje. My heart will triumph.*"

Mirjana told me, "I don't want to talk very much about the secrets, because secrets are secrets. I want to say one thing that is very important. Blessed Mary said, '*What I started at Fatima, I will finish in Medjugorje. My heart will triumph.*' **If the heart of our mother will triumph, we don't need to be scared of anything. It's only important to put our life in her hands and not to think about secrets. We should think about the messages and what she asked for us, so that we can help her Immaculate Heart to triumph.**"

Padre Livio told Mirjana in his interview with her that Mary, Queen of Peace, was coming to build us a new world of peace, the end of which is to bring us to the light of a closer relationship with God. Mirjana responded to him, "Yes, yes. I'm sure that eventually we will see this light. We shall see the triumph of the heart of Our Lady and Jesus."

Pope Emeritus Benedict XVI, then Cardinal Ratzinger, explained the meaning of the triumph of the Immaculate Heart of Mary in *The Message of Fatima*, May 13, 2000:

> The heart open to God, purified by contemplation of God, is stronger than guns and weapons of every kind. The *fiat* of Mary [her "yes" to become the mother of Jesus], the word of her heart, has changed the history of the world, because it brought the Savior into the world — because, thanks to her *Yes,* God could become man in our world and remains so for all time. The Evil One has power in this world, as we see and experience continually; he has power

because our freedom continually lets itself be led away from God. But since God Himself took a human heart and has thus steered human freedom towards what is good, the freedom to choose evil no longer has the last word. From that time forth, the word that prevails is this: "In the world you will have tribulation, but take heart; I have overcome the world" (John 16:33). The message of Fatima invites us to trust in this promise.

Pope Emeritus Benedict XVI offered a prayer on the Feast of Our Lady of Fatima:

> **[Mary], you promised the three children of Fatima that "in the end, my Immaculate Heart will triumph." May it be so!** May love triumph over hatred, solidarity over division, and peace over every form of violence! May the love you bore your Son teach us to love God with all our heart, strength and soul. May the Almighty show us His mercy, strengthen us with His power, and fill us with every good thing (cf. Luke 1:46-56). (Pope Emeritus Benedict XVI at Caritas Baby Hospital in Bethlehem, May 13, 2009).

The triumph of the Immaculate Heart of Mary means the triumph of goodness over the evil state of the world. It is the triumph of grace over sin, of faith over atheism, of love over hate, of virtue over vice, of life over death. It is the triumph of a loving motherly heart who wants to save her spiritual children on earth from evil and, by her intercession, obtain the grace from her Son, Jesus, for Him to do so, to reconcile them to Himself and to obtain a new era of peace.

The New Era of Peace

On July 13, 1917, Mary told the three children at Fatima, *"An era of peace will be granted to the world."* At the end of the century at Medjugorje, Mary said, *"Pray for peace so that as soon as possible a time of peace which my heart waits for impatiently, may reign."* (June 25, 1995). Sister Lucia of Fatima said, "The period of peace does not refer to civil peace." This peace is not merely the absence of external conflict. It is a positive interior quality, which is a gift from Jesus (see John 14:27). It is God's own peace, which is beyond all understanding. (See Philippians 4:7).

Mirjana said that when the first secret entrusted to her is realized, the power of Satan will be broken. (Connell, Janice. *The Visions of the Children*. New York, New York: St. Martin's Press, 1992, 1997). She explained that the century given over to Satan was generally the twentieth century, "part of which is in the twentieth century, until the first secret is unfolded."

The New Era of Peace will be a gift from God and not earned by human effort. This peace is not obtainable without responding to Mary's pleas. It is the peace that Blessed Pope John Paul II prayed for at the Basilica of Our Lady of Guadalupe, . . . "with the peace of God in our conscience, with our hearts free from evil and hatred we will be able to bring to all true joy and true peace, which comes to us from your Son, our Lord Jesus Christ, who with God the Father and the Holy Spirit lives and reigns forever and ever. Amen."

In 1995, Mary prophesied that a New Era would be announced by Blessed Pope John Paul II that would spring up after the purification of the earth. She said, "It is precisely through the sacrifice of this, the first of my beloved sons, [Blessed Pope John Paul II] that divine justice will be espoused to a great mercy. After the time of the trial, which will be one of purification for all the earth, there will spring up upon the world the New Era foretold and announced by him; and thus, in these final times, he invites you all to cross the bright thresholds of hope." (Mary to Father Stefano Gobbi of the Marian Movement of Priests, May 13, 1995).

On January 1, 2000, Blessed Pope John Paul announced this New Era. He said, "At the dawn of the new Millennium, we wish to propose once more the message of hope which comes from the stable of Bethlehem: **God loves all men and women on earth and gives them hope of a new era, an era of peace**. (Blessed Pope John Paul II, *Message for the Celebration of the World Day of Peace*, January 1, 2000).

Blessed Pope John Paul II described the New Era of Peace. He said, "I once more express my conviction, born of faith, that **God is even now preparing a great springtime for the Gospel**." (Blessed Pope John Paul II *Address to U.S. Bishops of Boston and Hartford*, September 2, 2004).

At a general audience on February 14, 2001, he said that **in the New Era brought by Christ, "God and man, man and woman, humanity and nature are in harmony, in dialogue, in communion."**

The Pope continued, "The authentic New Era is nothing other than the re-establishment of the lost relation between God and man. Christ must cancel the work of devastation, the horrible idolatry, violence and every sin that the rebellious Adam has spread in the secular affairs of humanity and on the horizon of creation."

"He 'recapitulates' Adam in Himself, in whom the whole of humanity recognizes itself; He transfigures him into son of God, He brings him to full communion with the Father," the Pope explained.

Christ's New Era, the Pope announced, also embraces "nature itself . . . subjected as it is to lack of meaning, degradation and devastation caused by sin," which will thus participate "in the joy of the deliverance brought about by Christ in the Holy Spirit."

We confidently await this New Era in hope.

5: How to Respond to Mary's Requests

How to Make a Good Confession

Mary's Requests

"*Make your peace with God and among yourselves. For that, it is necessary to believe, to pray, to fast, and to **go to Confession**.*" (June 26, 1981).

"*Pray, pray! It is necessary to believe firmly, to **go to Confession regularly**, and, likewise, to receive Holy Communion. It is the only salvation.*" (February 10, 1982).

"*Whoever has done very much evil during his life **can go straight to Heaven if he confesses**, is sorry for what he has done, and receives Communion at the end of his life.*" (July 24, 1982).

"***Monthly Confession will be a remedy for the Church** in the West. One must convey this message to the West.*" (August 6, 1982).

"*Do not confess through sheer habit, in order to remain the same after it. No, it is not good. **Confession ought to give life to your faith**. It ought to stimulate you and bring you back to Jesus. If Confession means nothing to you, really, you will convert with difficulty.*" (November 7, 1983).

Teaching

The Church's teachings on the sacrament of Confession are contained in the *Catechism of the Catholic Church,* (*CCC*), sections 1420 through 1484. Confession is a sacrament. A sacrament is a sign instituted by Christ to give grace. The sign is also the reality. The sign of Confession is the priest's words of absolution which also really absolve the sinner.

Jesus instituted the sacrament of Confession when He appeared to the apostles after His Resurrection and said, "Receive the holy Spirit. Whose sins you forgive are forgiven them, and whose sins you retain are retained." (John 20:23).

The sacrament of Confession is a gift of the mercy of God for the forgiveness of our sins. It reconciles us with God and His Church. In the sacrament, the priest acts in the person of Christ. He forgives the sins that we must confess and for which we are truly sorry and have a firm purpose of not committing again.

It is called the sacrament of Confession because the confession of sins is an essential element of it. It is also called the sacrament of conversion because it makes sacramentally present Jesus' call to conversion. It is also called the sacrament of Penance because it consecrates the sinner's personal steps of conversion, penance, and satisfaction. It is also called the sacrament of Reconciliation because it imparts to the sinner reconciliation with God and neighbor. Sin is above all else an offense against God, a rupture of communion with Him. At the same time, it damages communion with our neighbor and the Church.

During His public life, Jesus not only forgave sins, but He received sinners at His table, a gesture that expresses God's forgiveness and our reconciliation with Him. We should receive the sacrament of Confession regularly and at a bare minimum, at least once a year for mortal sins.

Practical Application

Come to Jesus in the sacrament of Confession. He waits there for you in the person of the priest to grant you His pardon and mercy. Jesus never wearies from repentant sinners or ceases from hoping for their return. The greater their distress, the greater His welcome. Doesn't a father love a sick child with special affection? Are not his care and solicitude greater? So is the tenderness and compassion of the heart of Jesus more abundant for sinners than for the just.

The mercy of the heart of Jesus is inexhaustible. The callous and indifferent should know that His heart is a fire which will enkindle them because He loves them. The measure of His love and mercy for fallen souls is without limit. He wants to forgive you. He is ever there, waiting with boundless love for you to come to Him. Do not be discouraged. Fearlessly throw yourselves into His arms! He is your father.

Only a baptized Catholic can receive the sacrament of Confession, unless there is a danger of imminent death of a non-Catholic Christian. Three things are required for a valid sacramental confession:

1. You must examine your conscience to be aware of your sins and you must confess them. What did you do wrong? How did you offend God and harm your neighbor? Go through the Ten Commandments in your mind to see how you might have violated them.
2. You must be sorry for your sins and be repentant with a firm purpose to amend your life, to sin no more and to avoid the near

occasions of sin – that is, the situations, persons and things that may lead you to sin.
3. You must complete the penance assigned to you by the priest as soon as possible. This is usually particular prayers, but sometimes it requires restoration of any harm committed such as returning or paying back for stolen or damaged property.

You should go to Confession at the regularly scheduled times or make a special appointment for a private confession with the priest. An appointment for a private confession is advisable for those who may take more time, because they have committed a sin which requires possible counseling or they have not confessed in a long time.

When you arrive for Confession, you should examine your conscience and wait your turn at the confessional. When you enter the confessional, choose either a face-to-face confession or an anonymous confession behind the screen. Begin by blessing yourself with the Sign of the Cross and saying, "Bless me Father for I have sinned. It has been __ (the number) weeks, months or years since my last Confession."

Then recite all of your sins and the approximate number of times that they were committed. You must confess all of the sins of which you are aware. Do not let fear or embarrassment of them hold you back from reciting them. The priest has probably heard them all before. Also, your confession is absolutely confidential. Under the Seal of Confession, the priest may never reveal your sins to anyone.

You may also ask the priest for advice regarding your sins. When you are finished, tell him that you are sorry for these sins and have a firm purpose to amend your life. Then the priest will briefly discuss the effects of your sins and will offer advice and encouragement on how to lead a better Christian life. He will give you a penance to perform and may ask you to say the Act of Contrition below. If you don't know it, simply say something like, "I'm truly sorry for my sins and I resolve to sin no more."

Finally, he will absolve you of your sins through a prayer. At the end of his absolution he will say, "I absolve you of your sins in the name of the Father, and of the Son, and of the Holy Spirit." Make the Sign of the Cross as he does this. He will then dismiss you by saying some variation of "go in peace." You reply, "Thanks be to God" and leave the confessional. As soon as possible, complete your penance and thank God that your sins have been forgiven!

Act of Contrition. *O my God, I am heartily sorry for having offended you. I detest all my sins because of your just punishment, but most of all because they offended you, my God, who are all good and deserving of all my* love. *I firmly resolve, with the help of your grace, to sin no more and to avoid the near occasions of sin. Amen.*

There is an iPhone application that aids in preparation for confession. However, it is not a substitute for the personal dialogue between the priest and the penitent required for the sacrament.

The name of the application is, "Confession: A Roman Catholic App." Its text received an Imprimatur from Bishop Kevin Rhodes of Fort Wayne-South Bend.

For more information: www.littleiapps.com.

How to Celebrate the Eucharist

Mary's Requests

"You do not **celebrate the Eucharist as you should**. *If you would know what grace and what gifts you receive, you would prepare yourselves for it each day for an hour at least.*" (1985).

"*There are many of you who have sensed the beauty of the Holy Mass.* **Jesus gives you His graces in the Mass.**" (April 3, 1986).

"Let the **Holy Mass be your life**." (April 25, 1988).

"**Mass is the greatest prayer** *of God. You will never be able to understand its greatness. That is why you must be perfect and humble at Mass, and you should prepare yourselves for it.*" (1983).

Teaching

The Catholic Church's teachings on the Eucharist may be found in the *Catechism of the Catholic Church* sections 1322-1405. The Eucharist is a sacrament instituted by Christ at His Last Supper. The Eucharistic celebration or Mass is a sacrificial meal at which we pray, listen to the Word of God and receive the Body and Blood of Jesus Christ, true God and true man, in communion with Him and one another. The Mass re-presents to us the Last Supper of Jesus and His sacrifice on the Cross.

All Catholics are required, under pain of mortal sin, to attend Mass on Sundays and Holy Days of Obligation. Prepared by the Sacrament of Confession, we must receive Communion at least once a year, preferably during the Easter Season. It is called "Mass" because it ends with our being sent forth (*missio* in Latin), so that we may fulfill God's will in our daily lives.

The Eucharistic celebration is both a sacrifice and a meal. It re-presents the sacrifice of Jesus Christ on Good Friday on the Cross to us in an unbloody manner. It also re-presents to us His Last Supper on Holy Thursday, the day before, where He gave His apostles His Body and Blood, in anticipation of

His offering on the Cross the next day, under the appearances of bread and wine. He told them to do that in memory of Him.

Sacrifice. In the times of the Old Testament, before Christ, God was really present in the sanctuary of the temple of the Jews in the Holy of Holies. This contained the Ark of the Covenant, which contained the manna from the desert, the rod of Aaron and portions of the Ten Commandment stones.

After the sacrifice of a lamb, its blood was sprinkled on the top of the Ark, which was called the mercy seat, in prayer for God's mercy for His people. The high priest was the only one who could enter the Holy of Holies and only on one day per year.

When Jesus was slumped, dying on the Cross, He shed His real Blood as the true Lamb of God, meekly, silently and innocently so that we would have the merciful forgiveness of our sins. The ultimate and perfect sacrifice was the giving of Himself to the Eternal Father for the forgiveness of our sins. He said, "It is finished, Father into your hands I commend my spirit." (John 19:30).

Now when we celebrate the Eucharist, Jesus re-presents to us His sacrifice on the Cross in a real but unbloody manner. We do not see His glorified body, but through a supreme act of faith we believe that He is really and truly present, Body and Blood, Soul and Divinity, under the appearance of bread and wine consecrated by the priest. It is called "Eucharist" because it is an action of thanksgiving to God.

Recipients of the Eucharist are not cannibals. Cannibals eat a dead person's body in a way that diminishes that person's body. Through the miracle of the Eucharist, we partake of the eternally life-giving glorified body of the very much alive Jesus Christ. Jesus said, "I am the *living* bread that came down from heaven. Whoever eats this bread will live forever; and the bread that I will give is my flesh for the life of the world." (John 6:51).

The celebration of the Eucharist is a mystery of faith. Miraculous things take place during the celebration that have eternal effects, ultimate worship of God is made and grace is poured out on those present and on those for whom the Mass is offered.

The Mass is not a new sacrifice of Christ because Jesus is now glorified at the right hand of the Father in heaven. Death no longer has power over Him. The Christ present at Mass is the glorified Christ, as He now is in heaven.

Because it makes present Christ's one sacrifice on the Cross, the Mass is both the source and summit of the Catholic life. At Mass, the Church does not become present at the foot of the Cross in sorrow but rather in joyful celebration, offering and partaking of Christ's Sacrifice.

The celebration of the Mass is the most important thing that the Church does each day. The Mass is a mystery of faith because it is an unbloody *re*-presentation of the presentation of the bloody sacrificial death of Jesus Christ on the Cross at Calvary two thousand years ago, which He anticipated and *pre*-presented to us at His Last Supper. The Eucharistic celebration is not a *repetition* of Calvary; it is rather making the unique sacrifice of Calvary *really present now* on the altar in an unbloody manner. By a sacrifice something is offered. If it is living, it is called a victim. In the Mass, Christ is both the victim and the priest, the same as on Calvary. He offers Himself by the actions of the priest who acts in the person of Christ and offers Himself to the Father in reparation for our sins.

Meal. At His Last Supper, Jesus celebrated the Passover Meal. The Passover Meal memorialized the original special meal that the Jews in Egypt ate, according to God's command, before their Exodus from the cruel Egyptian Pharaoh. The lamb was sacrificed and its blood sprinkled on their doorposts so that the angel of death would "pass over" them, but he would kill the first-born of the Egyptians. This was God's punishment upon the Egyptians in order to free His people from their slavery. That night the Jews ate the sacrificed lamb. That lamb died as a ransom, in place of the firstborn of the Jewish households who were saved from death. Thereafter, they celebrated the Passover Meal in memory of the Exodus and God's liberation of them from the Egyptian Pharaoh.

During His Last Supper Passover Meal, Jesus anticipated His sacrifice on Calvary and pre-presented it. He instituted the Eucharistic sacrifice when He gave them what appeared to be bread and wine and said, "This is my Body, This is my Blood." Then He told His apostles, the first bishops, "Do this in memory of me." (See Luke 22:19-20). So when the ordained priest says the words of consecration over the bread and wine, by the almighty power of God, the bread is transubstantiated (changed in substance) into the Body of Christ and the wine is changed into His Blood.

Jesus instituted the Eucharist in order to perpetuate His sacrifice on the Cross throughout the ages until He comes again, as a memorial of His death and resurrection. It is a sacrament of love, a sign of unity, a bond of charity, a Passover (Paschal) Meal in which Christ is consumed, the mind is filled with grace, and a pledge of our future glory in heaven is given to us. (*CCC* 1323).

Practical Application

You should gather together to celebrate the Eucharist in clothing and gestures that convey the respect, solemnity and joy of this moment when Jesus Christ presides represented by the priest and offers you His Body and Blood as our priest and victim.

The celebration of the Eucharist consists of the Liturgy of the Word and the Liturgy of the Eucharist. The Liturgy of the Word consists of readings from the Old Testament, the Psalms, the Epistles and the Gospels. In preparation for this celebration you should read and meditate on the readings of the Liturgy of the Word that will be presented at Sunday Mass. You should carefully and attentively listen to these readings and the homily proclaimed by the priest or deacon, to accept the Scriptures as the Word of God and to put them into practice.

You can read and meditate on these readings and the readings of the daily Liturgy. The Scriptures for each day may be found at the website of the United States Conference of Catholic Bishops: *www.usccb.org/nab/today.shtml*. They may be also found in the magazine *Magnificat*. You may subscribe at *www.magnificat.com*.

At the Offertory, you should offer yourself with Jesus to the Father, as a sacrificial gift along with the gifts of bread and wine that are presented. These will be changed through transubstantiation into his Body and Blood at the consecration by the priest. You sacrificially offer yourself in the hopes that you will be fully incorporated into the unity of His mystical body when you receive at Communion His real Body and Blood. You also offer gifts by donating to the collection.

No one may receive the Body and Blood of Christ unless he is a baptized Catholic, believes in the True Presence and lives the teachings of the Church. You must fast for one hour from food and liquids, except water, before receiving Holy Communion. You should not present yourself for reception of Communion unless you are in the state of grace.

If you are aware of serious, mortal sin, it must be confessed before a reception of Communion. You should refrain from reception of Communion until you have done so. Otherwise, you may be guilty of unworthy sacrilegious Communion.

St. Paul wrote, "Whoever, therefore, eats the bread or drinks the cup of the Lord in an unworthy manner will be guilty of profaning the Body and Blood of the Lord. Let a man examine himself, and so eat of the bread and drink of the cup. For anyone who eats and drinks without discerning the body eats and drinks judgment upon himself." (1 Cor 11:27-29).

As you approach the minister of Communion, you should show a sign of reverence, such as a bow from the waist, and say "Amen" after the Eucharistic minister says, "the Body of Christ" and receive with the option on your tongue or in your hand.

Then you may have the option to receive the Precious Blood, if it is available. Again, as you approach the minister of the Precious Blood, you should show a sign of reverence, such as a bow from the waist. After the Eucharistic minister says "the Blood of Christ", say "Amen", take the chalice, sip it and return it to the minister. Then you should return to your seat and make an Act of Thanksgiving to God.

How to Read the Bible

Mary's Requests

"*Dear children, today I call you to* **read the Bible everyday** *in your homes and let it be in a visible place so as always to encourage you to read it and pray.*" (October 18, 1984).

"*Every family must pray family prayers and* **read the Bible**." (February 14, 1985).

Practical Application and Teaching

The Bible is not just one book but a library of books. It consists of forty-five books in the Old Testament (before Christ) and twenty-seven in the New Testament (after Christ). The books contain history, wisdom, prophecy and prayers. "The Word of God is living and active, sharper than any two-edged sword, piercing to the division of soul and spirit . . . discerning the thoughts and intentions of the heart." (Hebrews 4:12).

The Bible is a sacramental, a sign of God's presence that is an occasion for grace. By reading it, you share in the very life of God. (See 1 Peter 1:4). He is with you when you read it prayerfully.

The Bible is the Word of God that you should read not as some human work of the past, but as His living Word which is ever timely and speaks to you personally. You should read the Bible prayerfully, with the lifting of your mind and heart in personal conversation with God who is the real Author.

God's Word in the Bible comes to you through human authors who wrote only what God intended for them to write. It is God's revelation of the truth that is necessary for your salvation. It should be received by your mind in accordance with the teachings of the Church, rather than your own private interpretation. It is not a science text that teaches how the world originated.

You must understand what the author is saying and how he is saying it. Is the literary form history, a real event, myth, parable, poem, prayer, vision or prophecy? What is the literal meaning? Is the literal meaning the real meaning? What is the figurative meaning? What is the spiritual sense (the allegorical, moral or heavenly sense)? What truth is the author trying to convey? Are you interpreting this in its context and according to its literary form and the teachings of the Church? How can you apply this truth to your own life?

A good reading program is to first read the New Testament Gospel of Mark. Then read the following Old Testament fourteen narrative and historical books, that will lead you chronologically through history from Creation to Christ: Genesis, Exodus, Numbers, Deuteronomy, Joshua, Judges, 1 Samuel, 2 Samuel, 1 Kings, 2 Kings, 1 Chronicles, 2 Chronicles, 1 Maccabees and 2 Maccabees. This will give you an overall understanding of the life of Christ and of our salvation history.

Then go back and reread more slowly. Meditate by using your imagination, placing yourself in the scene and experiencing the actions, motives and emotions of the participants. Ponder, listen, ask God questions, make a resolution to improve your life.

You can also read and meditate on the readings of the daily liturgy. They may be found on-line here: *http://www.usccb.org/nab/today.shtml*. They may be also found in the magazine *Magnificat*. You may subscribe at *www.magnificat.com*.

How to Pray

Mary's Requests

"**Pray, pray, pray.** *When I tell you this you do not understand it. Every grace is yours and you can receive them through prayer.*" (August 12, 1982).

"**Prayer is a dialogue with God.... Prayer is not a trifle.** *Prayer really is a dialogue with God.*" (October 20, 1984),

"*Dear children! You are a chosen people and God has given you great graces. You are not conscious of every message which I am giving you. Now I just want to say — pray, pray, pray! I don't know what else to tell you because I love you and* **I want you to comprehend my love and God's love through prayer.**" (November 15, 1984).

"*Dear children! Today again I call all of you to prayer. Only with prayer, dear children, will your heart change, become better, and be more sensitive to the Word of God. Little children, do not permit Satan to pull you apart and to do with you what he wants. I call you to be responsible and determined and to* **consecrate each day to God in prayer.**" (January 25, 1998).

Practical Application and Teaching

Prayer is the raising of our minds and hearts to God or the requesting of good things from Him from a humble and contrite heart, the hidden center of our being. (*CCC* 2559). One of His disciples asked Jesus, "Lord teach us to pray." (Luke 11:1). Jesus didn't give him a long explanation. He just prayed aloud and said, "When you pray, this is what to say." Then He taught them the Lord's Prayer.

In the Lord's Prayer we petition God for the holiness of His name, the coming of His kingdom, the fulfillment of His will, the nourishment of our lives, the forgiveness of our sins and our deliverance from temptation and evil.

Prayer expressions are vocal, meditative or contemplative. (CCC 2699). Vocal prayer is prayer of words said aloud or silently in our minds such as the Lord's Prayer or the Hail Mary prayer.

Meditative prayer is a quest of the mind to understand the why and how of the Christian life. Meditation engages thought, imagination, emotion and desire. Christian prayer tries above all to meditate on the mysteries of Christ. (CCC 2708). For example, you can pray the Rosary by imagining the mystery, placing yourself as a participant in it, reflecting on its meaning or message and have a silent interior dialogue with God.

Contemplative prayer is a quest from the heart for God alone. It is a gift that you can predispose yourself to receive in silence by quieting your mind and interior thoughts until you reach silent communion with God in humble faith beyond the senses. It is a gaze of faith fixed on Jesus, attentive to the Word of God in silent love. (CCC 2724).

You should pray because God asks this of you. He tirelessly calls you to this mysterious encounter with Himself. Prayer unfolds throughout the whole history of salvation as a reciprocal call between God and man. (CCC 2591).

You should pray so that you aren't put to the test. Jesus said, "Pray that you may not be put to the test. The spirit is willing but the flesh is weak." (Mark 14:38).

Jesus often retired to deserted places and prayed. (See Luke 5:16). He also said, "When you pray, go to your private room, shut yourself in and pray to your Father who is in that secret place, and your Father who sees all that is done in secret will reward you." (Matthew 6:5-6).

However, Jesus didn't mean to limit your places of prayer to deserted places and your private rooms. You can pray anywhere from the depths of your heart. Jesus didn't mean "your private room" only literally, but also metaphorically, as the room of your heart, the center of your being. Above all you should pray in the church, which is the proper place for liturgical prayer for the parish community and the privileged place for Eucharistic adoration. (CCC 2691).

You should pray to the Lord Jesus. Even though prayer is primarily addressed to the Father, you should invoke the name of Jesus by the power of the Holy Spirit. You pray in communion with the Blessed Virgin Mary because of her singular cooperation with the Holy Spirit. In this way, you magnify with her the great things the Lord has done for her and entrust your petitions and praises to her. (*CCC* 2680-2682).

You should pray constantly (see 1 Thessalonians 5:16-17) and at all times in the Spirit. (Ephesians 6:18). If you get tired, you should remember that Jesus often prayed all night. (See Luke 6:12).

"We have not been commanded to work, to keep watch and to fast constantly, but it has been laid down that we are to pray without ceasing." (1 Thessalonians 5:17). You should pray especially at turning points in your life. Jesus set the example and prayed when He chose the twelve to assist Him in His mission and when He entered into His passion.

You should pray as a person speaks to a friend. Moses spoke to the Lord face-to-face as a man speaks to his friend. (See Exodus 33:11). You should pray with the right heart in humility like the tax collector and not self-righteously like the Pharisee. (See Luke 18:9-14). You should pray with the Spirit who prays within you (see Romans 8:26); with your mind and spirit (see 1 Corinthians 14); with a right heart (see Acts 8:21-22); imploringly (see Luke 11); and without losing heart (see Luke 18:1).

Jesus taught His parable on praying with persistence to obtain loaves of bread from a friend for an unexpected guest. (See Luke 11). He taught you not to lose heart but to pray always like the widow to the corrupt judge. (See Luke 18:1).

You should pray in praise of God, in adoration of Him, in contrition for offending Him, in thanksgiving for Him and in petition to Him, especially for the coming of His Kingdom. You should pray for mercy (see Luke 8); for healing (see James 13:16); and for unity (see John 17). You should pray in intercession for the needs of others, especially for those who persecute you. (See Matthew 5:44). Jesus set the example for you and prayed, "Father forgive them, they know not what they do." (Luke 23:34). These general forms of prayer are explained in sections 2626 – 2643 of the *Catechism of the Catholic Church*.

You should pray through the intercession of the saints. They practiced heroic virtue and lived in fidelity to God's grace so they are proposed to you as models and intercessors. (*CCC* 828). "Being more closely united to Christ, those who dwell in heaven fix the whole Church more firmly in holiness. They do not cease to intercede with the Father for us, as they proffer the merits which they acquired on earth through the one mediator between God and men, Christ Jesus. So by their fraternal concern is our weakness greatly helped." (*CCC* 956).

You learn from the saints as models of holiness, particularly from the all-holy Virgin Mary, whom the liturgy of the Church celebrates in the rhythms of the Feast Days of the saints. (*CCC* 2030). Mary intercedes for you as she did at Cana when she asked her Son to meet the needs of a wedding feast. (See John 2).

You should try to make prayer a daily habit, especially the daily Rosary. You can begin this habit by praying at least one decade of the Rosary at a regular time and place. Then let this grow into the habit of the daily Rosary and, for those who are able, attendance at daily Mass which Mary calls "the best prayer."

How to Pray the Rosary

Mary's Requests

"*Recite the Rosary every day.*" (August 14, 1984).

"*Dear children, today I am requesting you to **start reciting the Rosary with deep faith**, so that I will be able to help you. You, dear children, wish to receive graces but you do not pray and I cannot help you if you do not want to make a move. Dear children, I urge you to **recite the Rosary so that the Rosary may become a task that you undertake with joy**; in this way you will understand why I have been with you like this for so long: I want to teach you how to pray.*" (June 12, 1986).

"*Dear children, again today I am urging you to pray and to abandon yourselves completely to God. You know that I love you and it is out of love that I come here to show you the path to peace and to the salvation of your souls. I want you to obey me and not to allow Satan to tempt you. Dear children, Satan is strong and that is why I ask you to pray, and to offer me prayers for those who are under his influence, that they may be saved. Be witnesses through your lives and offer up your lives for the salvation of the world. I am with you and I thank you. And then in heaven you will receive the rewards that I have promised you from the Father. Therefore, children, do not worry about anything. If you pray, Satan will not be able to put any obstacles in your way, because you are God's children and He keeps an eye on you. Pray! **Hold the Rosary constantly in your hands, as a sign for Satan that you belong to me.** Thank you for having responded to my call!*" (February 25, 1988).

Teaching

Mary asked St. Dominic to preach her Rosary to make his ministry more fruitful. In 1208, in Prouille, France, Dominic suddenly experienced an apparition of the Blessed Mother. She said, "*Wonder not that you have obtained so little fruit by your labors. You have spent them on barren soil, not yet watered with the dew of divine grace. When God willed to renew the face* of the earth, He began by sending down on it the fertilizing rain of the Angelic Salutation [the Hail Mary]. Therefore preach my Psalter [Rosary] composed of 150 Angelic Salutations and fifteen Our Fathers and you will obtain an abundant harvest."

The Blessed Mother was referring to the ancient origin of the Rosary, which got its start with monks who recited the 150 Psalms (Psalter), and gave the laymen who wanted to participate (but couldn't memorize the Psalms) pouches of 150 pebbles, so they could recite an Our Father on each of them. The laity next developed a rope with 150 knots, then strings with fifty wood pieces, and soon the technique spread to other parts of Europe, where the faithful began to recite a Hail Mary with each piece of wood. Finally, it took its present form with 50 small beads for the Hail Marys and five large beads for the Our Fathers in five decades each of the Joyful, Sorrowful, Luminous and Glorious Mysteries of the life of Christ.

Blessed Pope John Paul II wrote an Apostolic Letter, *On the Most Holy Rosary,* and said, **"To recite the Rosary is nothing other than to contemplate with Mary the face of Christ. . . . At the start of a millennium which began with the terrifying attacks of 11 September 2001, a millennium which witnesses every day in numerous parts of the world fresh scenes of bloodshed and violence, to rediscover the Rosary means to immerse oneself in contemplation of the mystery of Christ who 'is our peace', since He made 'the two of us one, and broke down the dividing wall of hostility.' (Ephesians 2:14)."**

Practical Application

The word "Rosary" comes from Latin and means a garland of roses, the rose being one of the flowers used to symbolize the Virgin Mary. It consists of various prayers prayed on beads, while meditating on "mysteries", which are events of Jesus and Mary. They are called "mysteries" because you can meditate on them but never fully comprehend them. There are four mysteries each of which contains five events. The mysteries are the Joyful, Sorrowful, Luminous and Glorious.

You should meditate on the mysteries as you pray ten Hail Marys which constitutes a decade. Each mystery has five decades. You meditate on the events by using your imagination and placing yourself in the scenes as a witness to the event and think of the actions and emotions of those involved.

Blessed Pope John Paul II said, "The Rosary is a prayer oriented, by its very nature, to peace. Not only because it leads us to pray it, supported by the intercession of Mary, but also because it makes us assimilate, together with the mystery of Jesus, His plan for peace. At the same time, with the serene rhythm of the repetition of the Hail Mary, the Rosary floods our spirit with peace and opens it to saving grace."

Rosary packages may be ordered from the Order Form.

Blessed Pope John Paul II said that this is how we should pray the Rosary:

> **Announce each mystery** to open up a scenario on which to focus our attention. The words direct the imagination and the mind towards a particular episode or moment in the life of Christ.
>
> **Listen to the word of God and** follow the announcement of the mystery with the proclamation of a related Biblical passage. As we listen, we are certain that this is the Word of God, spoken for today and spoken "for me."
>
> **Silence**. After the announcement of the mystery and the proclamation of the Word, it is fitting to pause and focus one's attention for a suitable period of time on the mystery concerned, before moving into vocal prayer.
>
> **Conclude** each mystery with a prayer for the fruits specific to that particular mystery. The Rosary is then ended with a prayer for the intentions of the Pope.

The Rosary Method

Make the Sign of the Cross and pray the "Apostles' Creed" while holding the Cross. (See all of the Rosary prayers on the following page).

Pray the "Our Father" on the first large bead.

Pray three "Hail Marys" on the next three smaller beads. Pray the "Glory be to the Father."

Announce the First Mystery; then pray the "Our Father" on the large bead of the first decade.

Pray ten "Hail Marys," while meditating on the Mystery on the ten small beads.

Pray the "Glory be to the Father" and the "Fatima Prayer", after each decade.

Before each decade, announce the next mystery followed by an "Our Father", on the large bead.

For each set of ten beads, pray ten "Hail Marys" on the small beads, while meditating on the Mystery.

After the Rosary, pray the Concluding Prayers.

As suggested by Blessed Pope John Paul II, the Joyful mysteries are prayed on Monday and Saturday, the Luminous on Thursday, the Sorrowful on Tuesday and Friday, and the Glorious on Wednesday and Sunday (except during Sundays of the Christmas season when the Joyful mysteries are prayed and the Sundays of Lent when the Sorrowful mysteries are prayed).

The Rosary Prayers

Sign of the Cross
In the name of the Father, and of the Son, and of the Holy Spirit. Amen.

Apostles' Creed
I believe in God, the Father Almighty, Creator of heaven and earth; and in Jesus Christ, His only Son, our Lord; who was conceived by the Holy Spirit, born of the Virgin Mary, suffered under Pontius Pilate, was crucified, died, and was buried. He descended into hell. On the third day He arose again. He ascended into heaven, and is seated at the right hand the Father. He will come again to judge the living and the dead. I believe in the Holy Spirit, the Holy Catholic Church, the communion of saints, the forgiveness of sins, the resurrection of the body, and life everlasting. Amen.

Our Father
Our Father who art in heaven, hallowed be Thy name. Thy Kingdom come. Thy will be done on earth, as it is in heaven. Give us this day our daily bread, and forgive us our trespasses, as we forgive those who trespass against us, and lead us not into temptation, but deliver us from evil. Amen.

Hail Mary
Hail Mary, full of grace, the Lord is with thee, blessed art thou amongst women and blessed is the fruit of thy womb, Jesus. Holy Mary, Mother of God, pray for us sinners now and at the hour of our death. Amen.

Glory Be
Glory be to the Father, and to the Son, and to the Holy Spirit. As it was in the beginning, is now, and ever shall be, world without end. Amen.

Fatima Prayer
O my Jesus, forgive us our sins, save us from the fires of hell. Lead all souls to heaven, especially those in most need of thy mercy.

Concluding Prayers:

Hail, Holy Queen
Hail, holy Queen, Mother of Mercy! Our life, our sweetness, and our hope! To thee do we cry, poor banished children of Eve; to thee do we send up our sighs, mourning and weeping in this valley of tears. Turn then, most gracious Advocate, thine eyes of mercy toward us, and after this our exile show unto us the blessed fruit of thy womb, Jesus. O clement, O loving, O sweet Virgin Mary

Verse: Pray for us, O Holy Mother of God.
Response: That we may be made worthy of the promises of Christ.

Our Father, Hail Mary and Glory Be for the intentions of the Pope.

Rosary Prayer
O God, whose only begotten Son, by His life, death, and resurrection, has purchased for us the rewards of eternal life, grant, we beseech Thee, that meditating upon these mysteries of the Most Holy Rosary of the Blessed Virgin Mary, we may imitate what they contain and obtain what they promise, through the same Christ, Our Lord. Amen.

How to Respond to Mary's Requests 97

The Rosary Mysteries

Joyful Mysteries of the Rosary

First Joyful Mystery: The Annunciation
"The Angel Gabriel said to Mary, 'Hail, full of grace, the Lord is with you. Blessed are you among women . . . . You shall conceive and bear a son, and you shall call his name Jesus. . . .' Mary answered, 'Behold the handmaid of the Lord, be it done to me according to your word.'" (Luke 1:28,31,38).

Second Joyful Mystery: The Visitation
"Elizabeth was filled with the Holy Spirit and cried out in a loud voice: 'Blessed are you among women, and blessed is the fruit of your womb. . . . The moment your greeting sounded in my ears, the babe in my womb leapt for joy.'" (Luke 1:42-44).

Third Joyful Mystery: The Nativity
"And it came to pass while they were there, that the days for Mary to be delivered were fulfilled. And she brought forth her firstborn son, and wrapped Him in swaddling clothing and laid Him in a manger, because there was no room for them in the inn." (Luke 2:6-7).

How to Respond to Mary's Requests 99

Fourth Joyful Mystery: The Presentation
"When the days of her purification were fulfilled they took Him up to Jerusalem to present Him to the Lord... Simeon blessed them and said to His Mother, 'Behold, this child is destined for the fall and for the rise of many in Israel, and for a sign that shall be contradicted; and thy own soul a sword shall pierce.'" (Luke 2:22,34,35).

Fifth Joyful Mystery: The Finding of the Child Jesus in the Temple
"After three days they found Him in the temple, sitting in the midst of the teachers, listening to them and asking them questions.... And He returned with His parents to Nazareth, and was obedient to them." (Luke 2:46,51).

Luminous Mysteries of the Rosary

First Luminous Mystery: The Baptism of Jesus
"Jesus came from Galilee to Jordan in order to be baptized by John. But John stopped Him saying, 'I have need to be baptized by You.' Jesus answered, 'Let it be so now, for by us must all righteousness be fulfilled.' Jesus arose from the water and behold, the heavens were opened and He saw the Spirit of God coming down like a dove, and alighting upon Him, a voice from heaven said, 'This is my beloved Son in whom I am well pleased.' " (Matthew 3:13-17).

Second Luminous Mystery: The Wedding at Cana
"At the wedding in Cana, they had need of wine and Mary, the mother of Jesus said to Him, 'They have no more wine.' Jesus said to her, 'Woman, what is that to you and me?' Mary said to the servants, 'Do whatever He tells you.' Jesus said to the servants, 'Fill the six stone water pots with water.' When this was done, Jesus told them to take some to the master of the feast. When this man had tasted it he told the bridegroom, 'Why have you kept the best wine until now?' This was Jesus' first miracle showing His glory and His disciples believed in Him." (John 2:1-12).

Third Luminous Mystery: The Proclamation of the Kingdom
At this time, Jesus began to preach and to say, "This is the time of fulfillment. The kingdom of God is at hand. Repent, and believe in the gospel."

"So I tell you, her many sins have been forgiven; hence, she has shown great love. But the one to whom little is forgiven, loves little." (Mark 1:14-15; Luke 7:47).

Fourth Luminous Mystery: The Transfiguration
"Jesus took Peter, James and John his brother and brought them up into a high mountain and was transfigured before them. His face shone like the sun and His clothing was white as light. And behold, there appeared Moses and Elijah talking with Him. A bright cloud overshadowed them and a voice said, 'This is my beloved Son in whom I am well pleased. Listen to Him.' As they came down the mountain, Jesus commanded them saying, 'Tell the vision to no man until the Son of Man has risen from the dead.' " (Luke 9:28-35).

Fifth Luminous Mystery: The Institution of the Eucharist
"When the evening came, Jesus sat down with the Twelve. And He said to them, 'How greatly I have desired to eat this Passover with you before I suffer.' And as they were eating, Jesus took bread and blessed it, and breaking it into pieces, He gave it to them saying, 'Take and eat; this is My Body which will be given for you.' After supper He took the cup and after giving thanks, He gave it to them saying, 'Drink you all of it, for this is the new testament in My Blood, which will be shed for you and for many for the forgiveness of sins. Do this in remembrance of Me.' " (Matthew 26:26-28).

Sorrowful Mysteries of the Rosary

First Sorrowful Mystery: The Agony in the Garden
"Kneeling down, He began to pray, 'Father if it be your will, take this cup from me, yet not my will but yours be done.' . . . In His anguish He prayed even more intensely, and His sweat became like drops of blood falling to the ground." (Luke 22:42-44).

Second Sorrowful Mystery: The Scourging at the Pillar
"Pilate released Barabbas to them. Jesus, however, he first had scourged; then he handed Him over to be crucified." (Matthew 27:26).

Third Sorrowful Mystery: The Crowning with Thorns
"Weaving a crown of thorns they fixed it on His head, and placed a reed in His right hand. To make fun of Him they knelt before Him saying, 'Hail, King of the Jews.' They spat on Him, and took the reed and kept striking Him on the head." (Matthew 27: 29-30).

Fourth Sorrowful Mystery: The Carrying of the Cross
"When the soldiers had finished mocking Him, ... they led Him away to crucify Him. On the way they laid hold of a certain Simon of Cyrene, coming from the country, and upon him they laid the Cross to bear it after Jesus." (Matthew 27:31, Luke 23:26).

Fifth Sorrowful Mystery: The Crucifixion
"When they came to the place called the Skull, they crucified Him. . . . Jesus said, 'Father, forgive them, for they do not know what they are doing.' . . . There was darkness over the whole land until the ninth hour . . . and Jesus cried out with a loud voice, 'Father, into your hands I commend my spirit.' " (Luke 23:33-34,44,46).

Glorious Mysteries of the Rosary

First Glorious Mystery: The Resurrection
"And looking up they saw that the stone had been rolled back, for it was very large. . . . On entering the tomb they saw a young man sitting at the right side who said to them, 'Do not be afraid. You are looking for Jesus of Nazareth who was crucified. He is risen, He is not here. Behold the place where they laid him.'" (Mark 16:4-6).

Second Glorious Mystery: The Ascension
"Then, after speaking to them, the Lord Jesus was taken up into heaven, and took His seat at God's right hand." (Mark 16:19).

Third Glorious Mystery: The Descent of the Holy Spirit
"And there appeared to them parted tongues as of fire, which settled upon each of them. And they were filled with the Holy Spirit and began to speak in foreign tongues, even as the Holy Spirit prompted them to speak." (Acts 2:3,4).

Fourth Glorious Mystery: The Assumption
"Arise, my beloved, my beautiful one, and come! . . .
You are all beautiful, my beloved, and there is no blemish in you." (See Songs 2:10; 4:7).

Fifth Glorious Mystery: The Coronation
"A great sign appeared in the sky, a woman clothed with the sun, with the moon under her feet, and on her head a crown of twelve stars." (Revelation 12:1).

How to Fast

Mary's Requests

"*The best fast is on bread and water. Through fasting and prayer one can stop wars, one can suspend the natural laws of nature. Works of charity cannot replace fasting. . . .* **Everyone except the sick, has to fast.**" (July 21, 1982).

"*I should like the people in this period to pray with me. And to pray as much as possible! In addition I want them to* **fast on Wednesdays and Fridays***, and recite the Rosary every day.*" (August 14, 1984).

Teaching

Fasting means to make a sacrifice to God, to offer not only our prayers, but also to make our whole being participate in sacrifice. We should fast with love, for a special intention, and to purify ourselves and the world.

"Jesus was led up by the Spirit into the wilderness to be tempted by the devil and He fasted forty days and forty nights." (Matthew 4:1-2). The season of Lent is a commemoration of Our Lord's fast, which He undertook before entering into His public ministry. It was a time of preparation for the tremendous mission that lay before Him. To do this, He denied Himself food during those forty days and nights.

Christian fasting is distinct from fasting in other religions because its objective is to imitate Jesus and to come closer to God, not ourselves. When we fast, we do not shut ourselves up inside, nor do we let it out and boast of our fasting. Rather, we unite ourselves with Jesus, who fasted in the desert. Our fast does not scorn the flesh, since the Son of God took that flesh upon Himself, becoming our brother. Depriving oneself and denying oneself are positive acts, which aim at the encounter with Christ.

The Church defines abstinence as meatless meals and a fast as one meatless meal per day, with two lighter meals, and no eating in between meals. Fasting only relates to solid food, not to drink, so any amount of water or other beverages may be consumed.

Abstinence from all meat is to be observed by all people 14 years and older on Ash Wednesday and on all Fridays of Lent. Fasting is to be observed on Ash Wednesday and Good Friday by all who are between 18 and 59 years old.

For those whose health or ability to work would be negatively affected by fasting and/or abstinence, the regulations above don't apply. If a Friday in Lent coincides with a solemnity, the abstinence is not required. The Bishop of a diocese can modify these rules for those in his diocese. For example, it is not uncommon to give dispensations from the normal Lenten regulations if St. Patrick's Day (March 17) falls on a Friday during Lent.

Since the Fridays outside Lent are specified as penitential days by universal church law, but abstinence is not specified by the Bishops of the United States, it is left to the individual to choose the form this penance takes. Pastoral teachings have urged voluntary fasting on other days during Lent and voluntary abstinence on the other Fridays of the year.

Practical Application

The teachings above are the minimal regulations. Because of the great evils of our time, Mary asks more of us. She asks for the best fast which is bread and water on Wednesdays and Fridays. Those unable or unwilling to fast on bread and water as Mary requested, can fast from meat or from enjoyments such as smoking, drinking, television, computer time, excessive work and play. You can also perform acts of mercy for others and give alms to the poor.

As Blessed Pope John Paul II said, "Jesus Himself has shown us by His own example that prayer and fasting are the first and most effective weapons against the forces of evil." (Blessed Pope John Paul II, Encyclical Letter, *The Gospel of Life*, 100). So let us pray and fast to avert the threatened chastisements.

How to Make the Total Consecration

Mary's Requests

"I would like to draw you closer to the Heart of Jesus. Therefore, dear children, I am asking you today to pray to my dear Jesus, in order that all your hearts may become His. **I also ask you to consecrate yourselves to my Immaculate Heart.** *I desire you to consecrate yourselves personally, as families and as parishes so that everything may belong to God through me. Therefore, dear children, pray that you may understand the true meaning of these messages that I give you. I do not want anything for myself, but all for the salvation of your souls. Satan is strong and therefore you, my little children, by constant prayer must draw close to my motherly Heart. Thank you for having responded to my call."* (October 25, 1988).

Teaching

The complete object of the consecration to the Immaculate Heart of Mary is the centrality of her being, symbolized by her physical heart, as the seat of her love, her interior perfections and her entire interior affective and moral life.

Blessed Pope John Paul II said at Fatima that "consecrating ourselves to Mary means accepting her help to offer ourselves and the whole of mankind to Him who is holy, infinitely holy; it means accepting her help – by having recourse to her motherly heart, which beneath the Cross was opened to love for every human being, for the whole world – in order to offer the world, the individual human being, mankind as a whole, and all the nations to Him who is infinitely holy." (*The Sun Danced at Fatima,* Joseph A. Pelletier, Image Books 1983, 204-205).

The Total Consecration was the personal spirituality of Blessed Pope John Paul II. His motto was *Totus Tuus (Totally Yours).* He wore the Brown Scapular sacramental as a sign of his consecration. We should imitate his example.

St. Louis de Montfort wrote, "Now, Mary being the most conformed of all creatures to Jesus Christ, it follows that, of all devotions, that which most consecrates and conforms the soul to Our Lord is devotion to His Holy Mother, and that the more a soul is consecrated to Mary, the more it is consecrated to Jesus. Hence it comes to pass that the most perfect consecration to Jesus Christ is nothing else but a perfect and entire consecration of ourselves to the Blessed Virgin." (*True Devotion to Mary,* 120). There is nothing new about this consecration, which St. Louis popularized. It has been practiced in the Church for over 900 years.

St. Louis explains that the most perfect practice of true devotion to Mary is the total consecration to her, (*True Devotion to Mary,* 118,120,121) by which we set aside ourselves to be used by her to accomplish her will, which is in union with her Son's. She in turn mediates our sacrifice to Jesus.

A chalice of itself is earthly material, but when a priest pours wine into it and consecrates it, the chalice becomes sacred and the wine is transubstantiated into the Blood of Christ.

So, too, are we mere earthen vessels (see Corinthians 4:7) but when we are totally consecrated to the Immaculate Heart of Mary, she mediates the new wine of grace to us and transforms us into something sacred, the image of her Son, so that no longer do we live, but Christ lives in us as one. (See John 2:3-10; Galatians 2:20).

Total Consecration and the Parable of the Widowed Mother

Once there was a rich father who died, willing all of his property to his only son. The son's obedience had merited this inheritance. He was a just steward of his inheritance and used it to support his widowed mother and her other children, whom she subsequently adopted.

Soon thereafter the natural son died, willing all of his inheritance together with what he had gained by his own merits, to his widowed mother.

His will named her as his executrix and trustee, as he trusted her to use his bequest for the benefit of herself and his adopted brothers and sisters.

On her part, the widowed mother simply carried out her son's will and dispensed his gratuitous bequest to her adopted children for their care and support.

On their part, the adopted children presented their needs to their stepmother, and were most grateful to their step-brother and step-mother for their generosity in caring for them as their own. They dedicated their lives to their step-mother and in love fulfilled her every request. In imitation of their step-brother, they gave from themselves to their step-mother for her distribution to all who were in need. Never was there a more charitable family.

In like manner, God the Father gave all graces to His obedient only Son, Jesus (see John 3:35), who merited them for our salvation. Jesus in turn, willed all of these graces and His own merits from the Cross to His Mother and named her as His Mediatrix, to dispense them according to His will to us, His adopted brothers and sisters (see Romans 8:16-17), for our sanctification and salvation. Mary follows her Son's will and dispenses all graces to us with tender, maternal love.

On our part, we should present our needs to our heavenly mother and express profound gratitude for her cooperation in her Son's redemption and for caring for us as her own. We express this gratitude best by imitating the Father and the Son in total self-giving and by fulfilling her request through our total consecration to her Immaculate Heart.

St. Louis de Montfort's Act of Total Consecration

O Immaculate Mother, I (Name), a faithless sinner, renew and ratify today in thy hands, the vows of my Baptism; I renounce forever Satan, his pomps and works; and I give myself entirely to Jesus Christ, the Incarnate Wisdom, to carry my cross after Him all the days of my life, and to be more faithful to Him than I have ever been before.

In the presence of all the heavenly court, I choose thee this day for my Mother and Mistress. I deliver and consecrate to thee, as thy slave, my body and soul, my goods, both interior and exterior, and even the value of all my good actions, past, present and future; leaving to thee the entire and full right of disposing of me, and all that belongs to me, without exception, according to thy good pleasure, for the greater glory of God, in time and in eternity. Amen.

How to Use Sacramentals

Mary's Requests

"I invite you to **place more blessed objects in your homes** and that each one wear some blessed object on himself. Let all the objects be blessed. For then, Satan will not tempt you so much, because you will be armed against him." (July 18, 1985).

Teaching and Practical Application

A blessed object is a sacramental, that is, any object over which an ordained clergyman (priest or deacon) has pronounced a blessing. The act of blessing sanctifies the object for use in prayer and devotion. The concept of blessing is prevalent in the Old Testament, where it is conceived as a communication of life from God.

A sacramental is a sacred sign that signifies spiritual effects that are obtained by the intercession of the Church. Sacramentals take various forms from blessings to blessed objects. The blessed objects of devotion most used by Catholics are: holy water, candles, ashes, palms, crucifixes, medals, rosaries, scapulars, and images of our Lord, the Blessed Virgin Mary, and the saints. Sacramentals do not confer the grace of the Holy Spirit in the same way that the sacraments do, but by the Church's intercessory prayer, they do prepare us to receive God's grace and dispose us to cooperate with it.

Just like with all sacramentals, there is no superstitious magical benefit derived from wearing a medal. The efficacy of sacramentals depends upon the devotion, faith and love of the person who uses them. As Christ was the invisible God made visible, so sacramentals, like sacraments, are visible signs of His invisible grace.

Sacramentals are sacred signs instituted by the Church. They prepare men to receive the fruit of the sacraments and sanctify different circumstances of life. (*CCC* 1677). Among sacramentals, blessings (of persons, meals, objects, and places) come first. Every blessing praises God and prays for his gifts. (*CCC* 1671). The medals of Jesus King of All Nations and Our Lady of America are special sacramentals for protection.

The front side of the Jesus, King of All Nations, medal shows His image in human form as the God-Man King. On the rim of the border are the words "O Jesus, King of All Nations, May Your Reign Be Recognized On Earth."

The reverse side of the medal shows the Eucharistic God-Man King in the form of the Sacred Host and the Most Precious Blood, with St. Michael the Archangel. Jesus revealed that around the border should appear the words, "At that time there shall arise Michael, the Great Prince, Guardian of Your People." (Daniel 12:1).

Jesus promised those who wear the medal "the grace of protection in times of harm and danger. This will especially be true of danger coming from natural disasters."

The front side of the medal of Our Lady of America shows her image, surrounded by the words, "By thy holy and Immaculate Conception, O Mary, deliver us from evil."

The reverse side of the medal shows the Coat of Arms of the Christian family, with the Triangle of the Trinity and the Eye of Divine Providence on the shield of the Precious Blood, through which sanctifying grace was made possible to fallen mankind.

The sanctification of the family through imitation of the Holy Family is represented by the Cross and the two lilies, on each of which is depicted a burning heart. The flaming sword is a symbol of Divine Love that is necessary for union with God, while the Rosary indicates our means of drawing close to the Holy Family through meditation on its mysteries.

The scroll above bears the inscription, "Gloria Patri et Filio et Spiritu Sancto", Latin for "Glory be to the Father and to the Son and to the Holy Spirit." Below that is the Latin, "Jesu, Maria, Joseph" for "Jesus, Mary and Joseph."

Sister Mildred, the visionary, said, "Those who wear the medal with great faith and fervent devotion to Our Lady will receive the grace of intense purity of heart and the particular love of the Holy Virgin and her Divine Son. Sinners will receive the grace of repentance and the spiritual strength to love as true children of Mary. As in life, so in death, **this blessed medal will be as a shield to protect them against the evil spirits**, and St. Michael himself will be at their side to allay their fears at the final hour." (*Diary* 17).

The sacramentals of the Rosary, the Brown Scapular and the medals of Jesus King of All Nations and Our Lady of America may be ordered from the Order Form.

6: Interviews

Interview with Visionary Mirjana Soldo by Father Tomislav Vlasic

This excerpt is from an interview on January 10, 1983 taken from the book, The Apparitions of Our Lady at Medugorje, *by Fr. Svetozar Kraljević. (Medjugorje, Bosnia-Herzegovina: Information Center "Mir" Medjugorje. 2005). It is edited by the author who deleted irrelevant material. Fr. Tomislav Vlasic is signified by "T" and Mirjana is signified by "M".*

T: Mirjana, we have not seen each other for some time, and I would like you to tell me about the apparitions of the Blessed Virgin Mary, and especially the events that are connected with you.

M: I have seen the Blessed Virgin Mary for eighteen months now, and I feel I know her very well. I feel she loves me with her motherly love, and so I have been able to ask her about anything I would like to know. I've asked her to explain some things about Heaven, Purgatory, and Hell that were not clear to me. For example, I asked her how God can be so unmerciful as to throw people into Hell, to suffer forever. I thought: If a person commits a crime and goes to jail, he stays there for a while and then is forgiven – but to Hell, forever? She told me that souls who go to Hell have ceased thinking favorably of God – have cursed him, more and more. So they've already become a part of Hell, and choose not to be delivered from it.

Then she told me that there are levels in Purgatory: levels close to Hell and higher and higher toward Heaven. Most people, she said, think many souls are released from Purgatory into Heaven on All Saints' Day, but most souls are taken into Heaven on Christmas Day.

T: Did you ask why God allows Hell?

M: No, I did not. But afterward I had a discussion with my aunt, who told me how merciful God is. So I said I would ask Our Lady how God could…

T: According to what you've said, then, it's as simple as this: people who oppose God on earth just continue their existence after death, and oppose God in Hell?

M: Really, I thought if a person goes to Hell… Don't people pray for their salvation? Could God be so unmerciful as not to hear their prayers? Then Our Lady explained it to me. People in Hell do not pray at all; instead, they blame God for everything. In effect, they become one with that Hell and they get used to it. They rage against God, and they suffer, but they always refuse to pray to God.

T: To ask him for salvation?

M: In Hell, they hate him even more.

T: As for Purgatory, you say that souls who pray frequently are sometimes allowed to communicate, at least by messages, with people on earth, and that they receive the benefits of prayers said on earth?

M: Yes. Prayers that are said on earth for souls who have not prayed for their salvation are applied to souls in Purgatory who pray for their salvation.

T: Did Our Lady tell you whether many people go to Hell today?

M: I asked her about that recently, and she said that, today, most people go to Purgatory, the next greatest number go to Hell, and only a few go directly to Heaven.

T: Only a few go to Heaven?

M: Yes. Only a few – the least number – go to Heaven.

T: Did you ask about the conditions for a person to enter Heaven?

M: No, I didn't; but we can probably say what they are. God is not looking for great believers but simply for those who respect their faith and live peacefully, without malice, meanness, falsehood.

T: This is your interpretation, your understanding?

M: Yes. After I talked to Our Lady, I came to that conclusion. No one has to perform miracles or do great penance; merely live a simple, peaceful life.…

T: Well, besides Heaven, Hell and Purgatory, is there anything else new recently?

M: Our Lady told me that I should tell the people that many in our time judge their faith by their priests. If a priest is not holy, they conclude that there is no God. She said: "You do not go to church to judge the priest, to examine his personal life. You go to church to pray and hear the Word of God from the priest." This must be explained to the people, because many turn away from the faith because of priests.

In our time, the Virgin told me, God and the devil conversed, and the devil said that people believe in God only when life is good for them. When things turn bad, they cease to believe in God. Then people blame God, or act as if he does not exist.

God therefore, allowed the devil one century in which to exercise an extended power over the world, and the devil chose the twentieth century. Today, as we see all around us, everyone is dissatisfied; they cannot abide each other. Examples are the number of divorces and abortions. All this, Our Lady said, is the work of the devil.

T: You have said that the devil has entered into some marriages. Is his rule limited to those marriages?

M: No. That is just the beginning.

T: This behavior of people – they're under the influence of the devil. But the devil does not have to be in them?

M: No, no. The devil is not in them, but they're under the influence of the devil, although he enters into some of them.

To prevent this, at least to some extent, Our Lady said we need communal prayer, family prayer. She stressed the need for family prayer most of all. Also, every family should have at least one sacred object in the house, and houses should be blessed regularly. . . .

T: Tell me where the devil is especially active today. Did she tell you anything about this? Through whom or what does he manifest himself most?

M: Most of all through people of weak character, who are divided within themselves. Such people are everywhere, and they are the easiest for the devil to enter. But he also enters the lives of strong believers — sisters, for example. He would rather "convert" real believers than nonbelievers. How can I explain this? You saw what happened to me. He tries to bring as many believers as possible to himself.

T: What do you mean, "what happened to me"? Is that what you talked about before?

M: Yes.

T: You have never discussed what happened into my tape recorder. Please try to describe it now, so I can record it.

M: It was approximately six months ago, though I don't know exactly and cannot say for sure. As usual, I had locked myself into my room, alone, and waited for Our Lady. I knelt down, and had not yet made the sign of the cross, when suddenly a bright light flashed and a devil appeared. It was as if something had told me it was a devil. I looked at him and was very surprised, for I was expecting Our Lady to appear. He was horrible — he was like black all over and had a… He was terrifying, dreadful, and I did not know what he wanted. I realized I was growing weak, and then I fainted. When I revived, he was still standing there, laughing. It seemed that he gave me a strange kind of strength, so that I could almost accept him. He told me that I would be very beautiful, and very happy, and so on. However, I would have no need of Our Lady, he said, and no need for faith. "She has brought you nothing but suffering and difficulties," he said; but he would give me everything beautiful — whatever I want. Then something in me — I don't know what, if it was something conscious or something in my soul — told me: No! No! No! Then I began to shake and feel just awful. Then he disappeared, and Our Lady appeared, and when she appeared my strength returned — as if she had restored it to me. I felt normal again. Then Our Lady told me: "That was a trial, but it will not happen to you again."

T: Did Our Lady say anything else?

M: Nothing else. She told me it would not happen again and that she would talk to me about it later.

T: You said that the twentieth century has been given over to the devil?

M: Yes.

T: You mean the century until the year 2000, or generally speaking?

M: Generally, part of which is in the twentieth century, until the first secret is unfolded. The devil will rule till then. She told me several secrets and explained them to me; and I have written them down in code letters, with dates, so I won't forget them. If, say, tomorrow a secret is to be revealed, I have a right, two or three days before, to pick whatever priest I want and tell him about it. For example: "The day after tomorrow, such-and-such will happen." The priest, then, is free to do as he thinks best with that information. He can write it out before it happens, then read it to others after it happens. He can also tell it to the people: "Tomorrow, such-and-such will happen." It's up to him to decide what to do with the information."

T: Were these secrets ever revealed before, to anybody in previous generations?

M: I can't answer that.

T: Since you've been told not to talk about them, I won't ask you to. That's all right — as it should be. But I'll ask you if you know when the secrets will be revealed.

M: I know. I know every date of every secret.

T: But you can't say anything about this?

M: I can't.

T: Can we suppose, then, that one of you might say that three secrets would be revealed before the great sign appears; then the rest of the secrets will be revealed, one by one? Is there anything to that?

M: Nothing like that, but something like this. First, some secrets will be revealed — just a few. Then the people will be convinced that Our Lady was here. Then they will understand the sign. When Jakov said that the mayor will be the first one to run to the hill, he meant that generally, people of the highest social class. They will understand the sign as a place or occasion to convert. They will run to the hill and pray, and they will be forgiven. When I asked Our Lady about unbelievers, she said: "They should be prayed for, and they should pray." But when I asked again, recently, she said: "Let them convert while there is time." She did not say they should be prayed for.

T: You can say nothing specifically until the moment Our Lady says you can?

M: Yes.

T: Can we say that some secrets belong only to you, personally?

M: No. None of the secrets is personally for me.

T: Not you, then, but Ivan has received personal secrets.

M: My secrets are for all mankind generally, for the world, Medugorje, some other areas, and about the sign.

T: The sign will pertain to this parish?

M: Yes, to Medugorje. But there is something else.

T: Something else?

M: Nothing for me personally.

T: You have been given the last of the secrets?

M: Yes, the tenth.

T: Can you tell me what it relates to?

M: I cannot; but I can tell you that the eighth secret is worse than the other seven. [Mirjana subsequently corrected this statement and said that it was the *seventh* secret that was worse and that was lessened.] I prayed for a long time that it might be less severe. Every day, when Our Lady came, I pestered her, asking that it be mitigated. Then she said that everyone should pray that it might be lessened. So, in Sarajevo, I got many people to join me in this prayer. Later, Our Lady told me that she'd been able to have the secret lessened. But then she told me the ninth secret and it was even worse. The tenth secret is totally bad and cannot be lessened whatsoever. I cannot say anything about it, because even a word would disclose the secret before it's time to do so.

T: I won't press you. Anyway, though, the tenth secret has to do with what will definitely happen?

M: Yes.

T: Unconditionally?

M: Yes, it will happen.

T: What does Our Lady say? Can we prepare ourselves for what will happen?

M: Yes, prepare! Our Lady said people should prepare themselves spiritually, be ready, and not panic; be reconciled in their souls. They should be ready for the worst, to die tomorrow. They should accept God now so that they will not be afraid. They should accept God, and everything else. No one accepts death easily, but they can be at peace in their souls if they are believers. If they are committed to God, he will accept them.

T: This means total conversion and surrender to God?

M: Yes.

T: After these ten secrets, after these eighteen months of apparitions, what do you tell the people they should do? What do you say to priests, to the Pope and bishops, without revealing the secrets? What does Our Lady want us to do?...

M: I say to all people: Convert! — the same as she said. "Convert while there is time!" Do not abandon God and your faith. Abandon everything else, but not that!

I ask priests to help their people, because priests can cause them to reject their faith. After a man has been ordained, he must really be a priest, bring people to the Church.

The most important point is that the people convert and pray.

T: What is the greatest danger to mankind? What does it come from?

M: From godlessness. Nobody believes — hardly anybody. For example, Our Lady told me that the faith in Germany, Switzerland, and Austria is very weak. The people in those countries model themselves on their priests, and if the priests are not good examples, the people fall away and believe there is no God. I heard of a priest to whom a rich man had left money to build a home for old people, but instead, the priest built a hotel. Now all the people in that city have turned their backs on the faith, because how could a priest not fulfill the last wish of a dying man and, instead, build a hotel and make money for himself? Nevertheless, people must understand that they shouldn't scrutinize a priest's private life, but listen to what he says through God — God's Word.

T: Why did Our Lady introduce herself as the Queen of Peace?

M: You know very well that the situation of the world is horrible. There are wars in every part of the world. The situation is very tense. Peace is needed — a just and simple peace. First, peace in the soul; then...

T: So the message of Our Lady is a message of peace?

M: Yes, primarily peace of the soul. If a person has it in his soul, he is surrounded by it.

T: Peace comes as result of faith in God and surrender to him.

M: Yes; as a consequence of prayer, penance, and fasting.

T: Our Lady tells us that peace can be achieved that way; but evil things will happen nevertheless. Why?

M: They have to happen. The world has become very evil. It cares about faith very little. A while ago, I told you what she said when I decided to wear a cross around my neck. How many city people will say with approval: "What a sensible girl", and how many will say instead: "How stupid she is"?

T: I do not remember your saying that to me.

M: Our Lady was telling me at length how faith has declined. For example, now I live in the provincial capital, Sarajevo, and if I put a simple cross pendant around my neck and walked on the streets, how many people would say, or think to themselves "What a sensible girl!" and what proportion would say or think, "What a stupid or old-fashioned girl"? Nowadays, people curse God, Jesus Christ, his Mother, his Father, day in and day out, habitually. Besides, people have fallen into very evil ways, so that they live in evil routinely. It's no wonder that God is at the end of his patience.

T: Why do you think the Blessed Mother always exhorts the world, over and over again, to prayer and penance?

M: When we pray, we pray to God. (That's what you said in your sermon last night.) In return, we receive peace of soul, tranquility. We have opened our hearts to God, so that God can enter and when we have God in our heart and soul, we cannot cause evil to anybody. We will not curse – do anything evil. We will do good.

T: But Our Lady also says that we should pray for others.

M: We have to pray for anyone we see who is — . For example, I always pray for nonbelievers, because they do not know what is missing in their lives. They have no idea of how much they may have to suffer later. I pray that God will convert them, that he will give then a sign, that he will open their souls so that they can accept the faith.

T: I understand that, with prayer, we open ourselves to God, but Our Lady always seems to stress the need of prayer for others — prayer and fasting. Do you think that prayer and fasting bring a proper balance into the world? Do you feel that prayer and fasting can even partially atone for all the sins of the world?

M: Yes, I do; it's possible. Much can be done through prayer and fasting. Our Lady has said that prayer can stop wars and prevent catastrophes. Prayer and fasting! Of course prayer can help a struggling human who does not accept God and religion. Moreover, we are obliged to pray that such a person's heart will be opened. Again, I talk to many nonbelievers in Sarajevo and try to explain things to them so that they will gain at least a little understanding. Sometimes, it is not their fault; they received no religious training when they were young. Or later, when they abandoned their faith, no one tried to help them. I pray that God will open such hearts.

T: How do people react when you tell them such things? Do they accept you and what you say?

M: Well, it is usually in the classroom when I talk to people. They do not know that Our Lady has appeared to me. But they soon discover that I'm a believer, because when I hear somebody curse God, I ask them not to do it, at least not in front of me. Then they ask me if I believe, and I tell them I do. That way, we start a conversation, and I try to explain things: about God, who he is, and what he wants us to do. They seem to understand what I'm saying. Many, in fact, ask me to write out a prayer for them so they can say it at night. Really, they accept what I tell them. Only last night, I converted a grownup, a man. When you do something like that, convert somebody, you've introduced them to the faith, and you feel you've done something very important. A great feeling of peace comes into my soul, a special joy. Somehow, your whole soul starts to glitter.

T: Have you received any special messages for priests and bishops?

M: No; but a long time ago, she said that they should accept us, help us as much as they can, and pray more and do penance.

T: Priests and bishops, too?

M: Yes....

T: Did you ever ask about other apparitions in the world — Our Lady's apparitions in our time at other places?

M: She mentioned a man in Germany who caused panic among the people — on buses, trains, and the like — telling them: "Convert! While there is yet time!" There are many false prophets in our time, she said, throughout the world, who lie, claiming to see Our Lady or Jesus. This is a great sin, and we should pray for such people. In fact, she and I prayed for fourteen days, exclusively, for false prophets. They do not understand how grave a sin it is to lie about having visions....

T: What is your habit of praying now, and do you have favorite prayers?...

M: I pray the Rosary and I pray for an hour or two, depending on how much time I have. But usually never less than one hour. I pray that God will give me the strength of soul that I can again think and behave normally. I also pray for unbelievers, for their conversion. And for the secrets....

M: When I pray, something comes to me, because I immerse myself in prayer. Then it's as if I'm speaking with someone. I express things in the way I think they should be said, all the while talking to God. Then I go back to saying the regular kind of prayers. Then I pray again in my own words. I say all this out loud. . . .

T: Do you know of any healing that's connected with you?

M: Yes, in Sarajevo. A man wrote to me that thank me.

T: What happened?

M: I had all that in Sarajevo. I wrote it all down in my notebook. He was in a wheelchair, unable to walk, and he wrote me a very beautiful letter, full of strong emotions, telling me about his suffering. I asked Our Lady to help him, and she told me that he is a firm believer but that he should pray more. He prays, but not for himself. And he should pray for himself, that he might be healed. Anyway, he finally prayed, and I prayed, and after three months he wrote to me again and said he could walk a little. He can get on his feet and walk a little with one crutch. He wrote to thank me.

T: So Our Lady said that if we pray for a particular need...

M: We should emphasize exactly that: Dear God, I'm praying to be healed of my illness. Pray like that. But pray away from your heart, from the bottom of your soul, with feeling. It does not have to be a "regular" prayer, but a conversation with God. "God, you see my suffering. You know how I am. I'm not complaining, my cross is not too difficult to bear; but I would like to be on my feet again so that I can move around in the world." Like that: conversation, then prayer.

T: How long should we pray?

M: I believe that sick people should speak and pray to God for one hour every day, intimately. I'm sure it would restore their souls and that God would grant them grace.

T: Did Our Lady ever recommend special devotions?

M: She always recommended faith, prayer, and penance. She never mentioned anything special for anybody, whether they were sick or healthy. But as I told you, she said we should direct our prayers: "I am praying for such – and – such." And we should pray with concentration, not race through the words of Our Father. The main thing is not to say the words of a prayer, but to feel them.

T: And fasting?

M: She said that sick people do not have to fast. If they do not fast, it is not a sin for them. They can do another good deed instead. For those who are able to fast, it is not enough that they do a good deed instead.

T: Does she say fasting must be on bread and water only, or are other kinds of fasting acceptable?

M: We did not discuss fasting except on bread and water. But probably she meant we should fast only on bread and water.

T: Everybody?

M: Yes — everybody who wants to receive something from God or have God's help.

T: Are there any other points you want to mention?

M: Not that I can remember.

Interview with Visionary Mirjana Soldo by Dan Lynch

I knocked at the door of the home of Mirjana Soldo, one of the Medjugorje visionaries, just in time for my 8:45 A.M. appointment with her on October 23, 2010. There was no answer. After a few knocks, a nervous and embarrassed Mirjana walked up behind me and said that she wasn't ready and needed a few minutes. Then she turned and started to walk quickly away. I called after her, "There's no need to hurry, I'm not going anywhere."

I saw a table on her front patio and arranged it for our interview. I cleared one half of the table and placed two chairs at the end so that we would face each other kitty-corner. She arrived shortly and I greeted her. [In the following, "D" is Dan, "M" is Mirjana.]

D. Good morning Mirjana. My name is Dan Lynch. I'm from America. Thank you for receiving me at your home.

M. I don't know why you wanted to see me. [With a quizzical look.]

D. Oh, I'm sorry, I thought that it was explained to you. I'm an author. I wrote this book. [Showing her the book.] It's called *The Ten Secrets of Mary*. You're the only visionary that I used as a source for the book. I've read everything that you said about the secrets. However, there are some conflicting reports about what you have said about the secrets and I would like to verify what I wrote in the book. I want to tell the whole truth.

D. Can we pray? [I raised my arms and prayed, "Come Holy Spirit, come by means of the powerful intercession of the Immaculate Heart of Mary, your well beloved spouse." We then prayed a Hail Mary together and I asked Our Lady, Queen of Peace, to pray for us.]

I'm from the state of Vermont. I'm married and have nine children and twenty grandchildren. I'm a retired judge and I've been in the Marian apostolate for over twenty years. I brought my wife and five of my children here to Medjugorje in 1988.

In 1994, in the middle of the war, I returned with 20 pilgrims to pray and fast for the end of the war. Father Svet and I led the pilgrims on a walking peace procession from Medjugorje to Mostar carrying the 6 foot high Images of Our Lady of Guadalupe and Jesus, King of All Nations.

I wrote this book primarily for the unbelievers, not to scare them, but to give them an incentive to convert and to believe. After the first secret happens, just the way it will be described three days in advance by Father Petar, the unbelievers and many others will want to know what they should do. My book tells them what Our Lady requests and how to respond to her requests.

I think that it will be like Pentecost, when the Jews who were gathered in Jerusalem heard the mighty wind of the Holy Spirit and asked Peter, "What should we do?" Peter answered them, "Repent, and be baptized every one of you in the name of Jesus Christ for the forgiveness of your sins; and you shall receive the gift of the Holy Spirit!" [Acts 2:37-38.] So, that's my background. Now can you tell me a little bit about your background and family?

M. I was born in Sarajevo and attended the University of Sarajevo for three years.

D. Did you get your degree?

M. No, it was impossible for me to continue my education because I could not receive permission from the Communist government. They knew me as a "visionary" and I was an enemy of the state which said, "God does not exist in Yugoslavia."

Both of my parents were born in Medjugorje and I used to come here to visit my grandparents when I lived in Sarajevo. The apparitions of Our Lady began here in 1981 while I was visiting. Later, I married my husband, Marco, and moved here in 1989. I have two daughters, Maria, who is now 19 and Veronica, who is now 16.

D. I won't ask you any questions about the details of the secrets or for you to violate any confidence with Our Lady. You know why?

M. Because a secret is a secret.

D. Yes, and do you know what Our Lady would do if I violated your confidence? She would slap me on the hand. [Slapping my right hand with my left as Mirjana laughs.]

M. I never ask Blessed Mary questions. I just listen to what she tells me. She told me, "Choose a priest to whom you will tell the first *secret*." She emphasized the singular. She did not tell me to tell him all the secrets. I chose Father Petar. I'll tell him the first secret ten days before it occurs. We will fast and pray together for seven days and then he will announce the secret three days before it occurs. I don't know if each of the secrets will be announced.

D. There are many reports that you had an apparition on October 25, 1985 and an interview with a priest (some say Father Petar) the next day in which you said that you were shown a vision of the first secret. You allegedly said that it was played before you as though it were a film and that Our Lady told you, "It is the upheaval of a region of the world." Could you tell me about that?

M. I did not have any apparition on October 25, 1985, I did not see that and I did not say that. [**D.** is wide-eyed and surprised.]

My last apparition of Our Lady was on Christmas day 1982, when she gave me the tenth and last secret. I had no apparitions after that except on my birthday [March 18] until 1987. Since then, I have received apparitions on the second of the month. Blessed Mary said that these apparitions are for "those who do not know the love of God yet." And we are not to judge who has or does not have the love of God. Right? You should know that since you are a judge. [Said with a smile.]

D. There are also reports that you said that the secrets involve what Our Lady herself described as "many horrors."

M. I did not say that.

On Christmas Day, 1982, I received the last of my ten secrets. Then Blessed Mary gave me all of the ten secrets. I received these ten secrets at the same time on one thing. It was like . . . [Mirjana pauses and looks up searching for words] what the Queens wrote on 150 years ago.

D. You mean a scroll?

M. Yes! Blessed Mary presented it to me and it contained all ten secrets and I could immediately read it.

D. I hope you have it in a safe place.

M. Yes, it's in my house.

D. Okay, could you please go in and get it for me? [Said facetiously as Mirjana laughs.]

M. It was in my house in Sarajevo during the war and was brought from there to here in Medjugorje for safekeeping. Others have seen it and can see something, but they see it differently. I showed it to one of my cousins who saw it as a letter asking for help. I also showed it to a friend who saw it as a prayer. Since then, I have not shown it to anyone else because different people see it in different ways, and only I see it as containing the ten secrets.

D. There are reports that you will give the scroll to Father Petar before the first secret, and he will be able to read it.

M. No, regarding my release of the first secret, Blessed Mary told me, "You will *tell* the priest ten days in advance." [Mirjana emphasized the word "tell" in contrast to the word "give".] Blessed Mary never told me to *give* him the scroll. My only role is to tell Father Petar. My role is not to distribute the secrets to the world.

D. Do each of you six visionaries have the same secrets?

M. We visionaries do not talk to each other about the secrets, so we don't know if we have the same secrets or not.

D. Is the sign one of the secrets or not?

M. It may or may not be a secret. I can't tell you.

D. There are conflicting reports about who the secrets are for. Some reports say that some of the secrets are for the Church and some for your parish. Who are the secrets for? Are some for the parish? Some for the Church or the world or what?

M. All of the secrets are for all of the world, none are just for the parish or the Church.

D. There are conflicting reports about which secret was lessened. Was it the seventh secret or the eighth secret that was lessened through prayer?

M. It was the seventh secret, not the eighth secret. After the seventh secret was lessened, Blessed Mary told me, "Never ask this again." So I have not asked for any other secrets to be lessened.

Why can't the secrets be beautiful? Blessed Mary gives us hope.

Now I really must go, I need to prepare lunch for the pilgrims staying here.

D. Oh, I'm sorry, I can come back. Duty first!

M. No, I'm sorry, I'm leaving tomorrow for Italy and have to get ready.

D. Oh, well, [stammering and caught off guard] would you please give us a summary statement about the secrets?

M. I don't want to talk very much about the secrets, because secrets are secrets. I want to say one thing that is very important. Blessed Mary said, "What I started at Fatima, I will finish in Medjugorje. My heart will triumph."

If the heart of our mother will triumph, we don't need to be scared of anything. It's only important to put our life in her hands and not to think about secrets. We should think about the messages and what she asked for us, so that we can help her Immaculate Heart to triumph.

D. So the most important thing is to respond to her requests for conversion, faith, prayer and fasting and not to be fearful of any secrets?

M. Yes, look at us visionaries. Look at me. I am always joking, smiling, living my life with God and Blessed Mary with hope, because my faith is hope. I hope in God's love. I hope that He will judge me with love, I don't think about secrets.

D. And the *Catechism of the Catholic Church* defines hope as "the confident expectation of divine blessing." [CCC 2090]. Do you have that confidence? That we will receive God's blessing?

M. Yes, yes, because God is my Father and He loves us and He sends His mother for so many years here to Medjugorje to help us to find Jesus, to find a good way, where we will meet Jesus and have real peace.

D. Is there anything else that you'd like to add?

M. Yes. I want to ask everybody to pray for those who do not recognize the love of God yet. Because when we pray for them, we pray for us, for our future, because who of us can say, "I am a good believer, I'm doing everything that God wants"? And when we pray for them, we pray for us.

D. And that's why I wrote this book, *The Ten Secrets of the Blessed Virgin Mary*, not to scare people but to help them to prepare for them so that they don't happen or they don't happen severely, because they convert and believe and pray and fast like Our Lady has asked us to do.

M. That's very good that you wrote the book not to scare people. This is important because a mother never scares her children and never gives them a reason to be afraid. She gives them hope and love. Blessed Mary is not coming to Medjugorje so that we are afraid of the future, but so that we have love and peace in the future with her.

D. So you hope that my book gives people hope?

M. I will pray.

D. Father Petar says, "Everything is closer and closer, God has to do something very quickly." Would you comment on that?

M. We can comment in many ways, but, maybe I'll be in front of God tomorrow. I won't have time to wait for secrets, I must change myself today. I always tell the pilgrims, "Don't talk about secrets, don't think about secrets, think of yourself, think of today, where are you today with God? Because you don't know what you will have tomorrow."

D. Thanks very much for seeing me Mirjana, can we get our picture taken?

M. Yes, of course.

7: The Status of the Church's Ruling on Medjugorje

The status of the Church's ruling on the apparitions and revelations from Medjugorje is based upon a decision made by the then Yugoslavian Bishops' Conference on April 10, 1991. In 1987, Cardinal Joseph Ratzinger (later Pope Emeritus Benedict XVI) entrusted the investigation into their hands. They ruled that, on the basis of the investigations to that date, "it cannot be affirmed that one is dealing with supernatural apparitions and revelations."

However, the implication is that it also cannot be affirmed that one is *not* dealing with supernatural apparitions and revelations. There has been no further ruling on them since April 10, 1991. They are neither approved nor disapproved by the Church.

After that date, Serbia attacked Slovenia and a war broke out. The war resulted in the dissolution of the nation of Yugoslavia and the Bishops' Conference of Yugoslavia. The Holy See stated, "Since the division of Yugoslavia into different independent nations it would now pertain to the members of the Episcopal Conference of Bosnia-Hercegovina to eventually reopen the examination of this case, and to make any new pronouncements that might be called for."

However, the Episcopal Conference of Bosnia-Hercegovina never made any new pronouncements. So, in 2010 the Vatican itself formed a new investigative commission to report to the Congregation for the Doctrine of the Faith which will decide the case.

Bishop Ratko Peric is the present Bishop of the Diocese of Mostar, in which Medjugorje is located. He does not believe in the apparitions and messages and is opposed to the spreading of the messages. He declared that it was his position that the apparitions or revelations were definitely not supernatural. However, this is only his personal opinion and it is not binding on anyone. His negative comments about Medjugorje were addressed directly in 1998 by the Congregation for the Doctrine of the Faith, which sent a letter to Bishop Gilbert Aubry, Bishop of Saint-Denis de la Reunion, clarifying its position on Medjugorje.

The Congregation, at that time, was presided over by Cardinal Joseph Ratzinger, later Pope Emeritus Benedict XVI. Its letter said that Bishop Peric's opinion "should be considered the expression of the personal conviction of the Bishop of Mostar which he has the right to express as Ordinary of the place, but which is and remains his personal opinion."

The letter also stated, "Finally, as regards pilgrimages to Medjugorje, which are conducted privately, this Congregation points out that they are permitted on condition that they are not regarded as an authentification of events still taking place and which still call for an examination by the Church."

Professor and Mariologist, Dr. Mark Miravalle, wrote in the book, *Are the Medjugorje Apparitions Authentic* (Hiawasee, Georgia, New Hope Press, 2008):

> The Medjugorje apparitions possess all the principal characteristics that the Church looks for in manifesting supernatural authenticity. The message contents are in complete conformity with the official doctrinal teachings of the Catholic Church. The phenomena that accompany the messages constitute scientifically validated ecstasy during the apparitions and numerous reports of healings. The visionaries manifest lives of moral integrity and psychological stability. The spiritual fruits from the apparitions have also had a monumental worldwide effect of conversions, returns to the Church and to proper states in life, as well as an extraordinary number of vocations to the priesthood and religious life.
>
> Further credibility is added by the fact that more than 200 Bishops, Archbishops and Cardinals have visited the site officially, in addition to the many unofficial visits by the shepherds of the Church. In addition, well over 100 Bishops, Archbishops and Cardinals have publicly expressed their belief in Our Lady's presence in Medjugorje. The spiritual fruits of conversion and spiritual peace have been the ubiquitous testimony of the greater part of the forty million pilgrims who have come to Medjugorje and have responded to the Queen of Peace's call for greater faith, prayer, fasting, conversion, and peace.

Austrian Cardinal Christopher Schönborn made a pilgrimage to Medjugorje from December 28, 2009 to January 2, 2010. Cardinal Schönborn is a former student and personal friend of Pope Emeritus Benedict XVI. He is the President of the Austrian Bishops' Conference and a member of the Congregation on the Doctrine of the Faith. He is well known for his work as editorial secretary of the *Catechism of the Catholic Church*, his contributions to the Pontifical Theological Commission and his numerous scholarly publications.

Cardinal Schönborn summarized the status of the Church's ruling on Medjugorje and said that the Holy See, in accordance with the Statement of Bishops from 1991, says the following:

> First: *Non constat de supernaturalitatae*. That is an expression that is rarely used and means that the supernaturality of the events has not been confirmed. That is a classical formulation of the Church doctrine. It is not said that the supernaturality was excluded, but has not, or still is not finally confirmed, and all because of one simple reason that I fully support. I am a member of the Congregation for the Doctrine of the Faith, and it is understandable that I support that if we were to discuss it. Namely, as long as the phenomenon is still ongoing, it is normal that the final decision of the Church is not going to take place yet, because something like that was never done in the past. Both in Lourdes and Fatima, the events first ceased and then the Church made its decision about that; its final decision. Sooner or later that will take place here as well, but until then we leave the Mother of God with freedom of choice.
>
> Second: No official pilgrimages are to be organized, which means that I cannot organize a pilgrimage of my diocese to Medjugorje. That is logically related to what was mentioned in the previous point. So, there is no official recognition yet, but in that formulation it is also said that supernaturality is not excluded. The Church has clearly said it is not excluded. It is not confirmed, but it is not excluded.
>
> Third: Church doctrine is clearly in accordance with the statement of the Yugoslavian Bishops that the faithful journeying to Medjugorje require attention and pastoral care. That means that indeed pastoral care of pilgrims needs to exist, and that is the matter that many are trying to serve. *Gebesaktion Wien*, amongst others, who take care of pilgrims, follow them and help them even after pilgrimages. I think in that way, Medjugorje pilgrims can continue well on their journey, with full trust that the Church, Mother and Teacher, in this case, is going to continue to monitor their journey. I would advise patience. The Mother of God is so patient with us that for nearly 29 years here, in a very direct way, she is showing her closeness and care for the parish of Medjugorje and numerous pilgrims. We can peacefully wait and have patience! Twenty-nine years is a long period of time for us, but not such a long period for our God!

On March 17, 2010, the Vatican announced that it formed a commission to investigate the phenomenon of Medjugorje. A short communique issued by the Vatican press office indicated that, "An international investigative commission on Medjugorje has been constituted, under the presidency of Cardinal Camillo Ruini and dependent upon the Congregation for the Doctrine of the Faith. Said commission — made up of cardinals, bishops, specialists and experts — will work privately, submitting the results of its work to the authority of the Congregation."

The press office explained, "it is not the Commission itself that makes the decisions, the definitive pronouncements, but it offers the result of its study, its 'vote', as it is referred to in technical terms, to the Congregation, which will then decide on the case."

The Church has made few judgments on the many apparition claims in history. Father Salvatore Perrella, assistant dean at the Pontifical Theological Faculty Marianum said, "It's not always possible to ascertain if they are true or false because the phenomenon is much bigger than us."

Father Perella is a theologian who also serves as an expert for the Congregation for the Doctrine of the Faith. He is also a member of the Commission formed to study the Medjugorje apparitions. In a statement in January 2011, he said, "The Pope wants a decisive conclusion made," adding that it will be a very long process.

The case under study "is a serious thing" that is "very complex", though not impossible to resolve, Father Perella said. Although the visionaries have claimed to see apparitions of Mary at Medjugorje for the past 30 years, such an extended duration of alleged apparitions in one place is no longer "something that generates suspicion," he said. That's because there are similar precedents such as the apparitions of Our Lady of Laus, France, which occurred during the 17th century and lasted for 54 years, but did not receive formal Church recognition until 2008.

The process of the Commission will be slow and the probable results will not be a statement on the "supernatural nature" of the apparitions or messages, but rather a clarification of the judgment that the former Yugoslavian Bishops made in 1991 and a clear, precise and authoritative guide for pilgrims to the parish.

The Commission will probably simply determine that there is no evidence of fraud, trickery, or diabolical action and that the visionaries are psychologically sound. The Church has never pronounced a judgment of approval on a case of apparitions that are still in progress, as they are in Medjugorje, but it will guide the faithful in their devotion.

Appendices

A. The Prayers for Protection of the Jesus, King of All Nations, Devotion and Angel Protection Prayers

The Jesus, King of All Nations, Devotion is a helpful aid for us to convert and to prepare for and protect against chastisements. The Devotion was granted the *Nihil Obstat* which is a declaration that is free of doctrinal or moral error.

Jesus revealed His only medal in the world and promised us protection if we wore it. Jesus also promised us graces of forgiveness, conversion, healing and peace, through the practice of the Devotion. The Devotion is practiced by the wearing of the medal; veneration of His Image; adoration of the Blessed Sacrament; the reception of the sacraments of Penance and the Eucharist and the recitation of the prayers that he revealed. These prayers are contained below.

The Novena in Honor of Jesus as True King

This simple Novena is a most generous gift from Our Lord. Jesus gave these extraordinary promises: "*I promise you that every time you say these Novena prayers I will convert ten sinners, bring ten souls into the One True Faith, release ten souls from Purgatory, many of whom are the souls of priests,* **and be less severe in My judgment of your nation.**"

The Novena consists of praying once a day over a period of nine days a set of one OUR FATHER, one HAIL MARY and one GLORY BE, recited along with the following Novena Prayer:

> O Lord our God, You alone are the Most Holy King and Ruler of all nations. We pray to You, Lord, in the great expectation of receiving from You, O Divine King, mercy, peace, justice and all good things.
>
> Protect, O Lord our King, our families and the land of our birth. Guard us, we pray, Most Faithful One! Protect us from our enemies and from Your Just Judgment.
>
> Forgive us, O Sovereign King, our sins against You. Jesus, You

are King of Mercy. We have deserved Your Just Judgment. Have mercy on us, Lord, and forgive us. We trust in Your Great Mercy.

O most awe-inspiring King, we bow before You and pray; may Your Reign, Your Kingdom, be recognized on earth! Amen.

Novena of Holy Communions

This Novena consists of offering nine consecutive Holy Communions in honor of Jesus, King of All Nations. Jesus said, *"I desire that the faithful souls who embrace this devotion to Me.... make a Novena of Holy Communions. They therefore shall offer me nine (9) consecutive Holy Communions, and go to Confession during this Novena, if possible, in honor of Me as 'Jesus, King of All Nations'."*

Jesus indicated that by "consecutive", He meant nine Communions, one after another, that the soul would receive. They need not be on nine calendar days in a row, just <u>each</u> Communion received, one after the other.

The powerful and unprecedented effects of this Novena were shown to Jesus' "Secretary" in a vision. She saw Jesus gazing up to Heaven. Nine times He gave a command and an angel came to earth. Jesus explained: *"My daughter, for those souls who will offer Me [this] devotion, I will bid an angel of each of the Nine Choirs, one with each Holy Communion, to guard this soul for the rest of its life on this earth."*

Jesus wants us to pray the Novena for others, and explains its necessity at this time: *"This Novena may be prayed with its promises for another soul, and that soul will also receive additional* **angelic protection**. *I urge My faithful ones to offer Me this Novena again and again so that I may continue to send down My holy angels for the protection and assistance of other souls who cannot do this for themselves.* **In these end-times, the power of the enemy has greatly increased. I see how greatly My children are in need of My protection."**

In His great generosity, Jesus granted that, in addition to the angelic protection, one may have a separate, unrelated intention for this Novena. He promised: *"What they ask for in this Novena, if it be according to My Most Holy Will, I will surely grant it. Let these souls ask from Me without reservation."*

The Chaplet of Unity

Jesus spoke these words and promises concerning the Chaplet of Unity:

*I, Jesus, Son of the Most High God, Who AM Sovereign LORD, promise to hold out to the souls who pray My Chaplet of Unity the Scepter of My Kingship and **grant them Mercy, Pardon, and Protection in times of severe weather and plagues. I extend this promise not only for yourselves, but also for individuals for whom you pray. No, My beloved, sin and evils committed by mankind are too great, no longer will I spare My judgment to correct the conscience of mankind as a whole, but this devotion and Chaplet prayed with repentance, confidence, and love, will heal, save, and unite souls to My Mercy who otherwise would be lost. Any harm or danger, spiritual or physical, whether it be to soul, mind or body, will I protect these souls against, and clothe them over with My Own mantle of Kingly Mercy.** To this I add the promise of the assistance of My Most Holy Mother's mediation on their behalf. Even if you die, you shall not be lost, for you shall know salvation and union with Me in the Kingdom of My Father, where We reign with the Holy Spirit, eternally the Divine Trinity, One God.*

The Chaplet is recited on ordinary Rosary beads. Groups may divide the recitation between Leader (L) and Responders (R). If you are alone, recite both parts. Recite on the large bead before each of five decades:

L: God our Heavenly Father, through Your Son Jesus, our Victim-High Priest, True Prophet, and Sovereign King,

R: Pour forth the power of Your Holy Spirit upon us and open our hearts. In Your Great Mercy, through the Motherly Mediation of the Blessed Virgin Mary, our Queen, forgive our sinfulness, heal our brokenness, and renew our hearts in the faith, and peace, and love, and joy of Your Kingdom, that we may be one in You.

Recite on the ten small beads of each of the five decades:

L: In Your Great Mercy,

R: Forgive our sinfulness, heal our brokenness, and renew our hearts that we may be one in You.

Conclude in unison:

Hear, O Israel! The Lord Our God is One God!

Oh Jesus, King of All Nations, may Your reign be recognized on Earth!

Mary, Our Mother and Mediatrix of All Grace, pray and intercede for us your children!

Saint Michael, great prince and guardian of your people, **come with the holy angels and saints and protect us!**

Saint Michael the Archangel

Saint Michael the Archangel,
defend us in battle.
Be our protection against the wickedness and snares of the devil.
May God rebuke him, we humbly pray;
and do Thou, O Prince of the Heavenly Host —
by the Divine Power of God —
cast into hell, Satan and all the evil spirits,
who roam about the world seeking the ruin of souls. Amen.

Guardian Angel

Angel of God, my guardian dear, To whom God's love
commits me here,
Ever this day, be at my side,
To light and guard,
To rule and guide. Amen.

B. The I Can Do This! Checklist for the Laity

Many people ask what can *I* do in the New Evangelization as requested by Blessed Pope John Paul II.

As a member of the lay faithful, you are called by your Baptism to be an apostle to bring the Gospel message into the real world, such as your family, neighborhood, work, parish, community, the media, politics, sports, etc.

You are part of the priesthood of the laity who offer, by means of the hands of the priest in the Eucharist, Christ's Body and Blood, Soul and Divinity with your entire existence, as praise and thanksgiving to God, as intercessors for the needs of the world and in reparation and atonement for your sins and the sins of the whole world.

The Eucharist must be the source and summit of your Christian life. This leads to what St. Josemaría Escriva called a "priestly soul and a lay mentality." From this Eucharistic source, you can propose the Gospel message as the best way to solve the personal and social problems of our times, as the best way to seek peace and justice in the family and among peoples, and as the best way to build what Blessed Pope John Paul II called "a Culture of Life and a Civilization of Love."

As a Lay Apostle, you are special in God's plan for the New Evangelization. Your mission is to allow the Sacred Heart of Jesus to flow through you, as one of His arteries, to bring His grace, mercy and love to His body, the Church.

You can be a Lay Apostle! You don't need any special education or training. Just be yourself, and practice your faith, hope and love. But you can do more than you are doing now. You can do this:

1. Be Holy! Be personally holy, according to your state in life as a husband, wife, mother, father, daughter, son, sister, brother or single person.

2. Love one another and your enemies. Forgive those who have hurt you. Be kind and gentle to others and respectful of them.

3. Pray the daily Rosary and the Chaplet of Unity.

4. Consecrate yourself to the Immaculate Heart of Mary and wear the Brown Scapular as a sign of your consecration.

5. Wear the medals of protection of Our Lady of America and Jesus, King of All Nations. (See Chapter 5).

6. Sacrifice through fasting on bread and water on Wednesdays and Fridays, if you are able, or make other acts of self-denial, such

as renouncing addictive behavior of watching television, using computers, smoking, drinking, etc.

7. Practice the First Friday Devotion of attending Mass and receiving Communion on nine First Fridays of the month in reparation for the offenses committed against the Sacred Heart of Jesus.

8. Practice the First Saturday Devotion of praying the Rosary, meditating for fifteen minutes on the mysteries, attending Mass and receiving Holy Communion, in reparation for the offenses committed against the Immaculate Heart of Mary, on five First Saturdays of the month with confession within eight days of each First Saturday.

9. Practice Holy Hours of adoration of the Blessed Sacrament and make visits to the Blessed Sacrament.

10. Learn the Catholic Church's teachings on faith and morals by reading the *Catechism of the Catholic Church* and the Scriptures.

11. Practice apostolic action such as:
    - Be a missionary to the culture by speaking and writing seeds of truth in your own environment to family, neighbors, friends and co-workers. You may be the only Gospel that someone ever sees or hears!
    - Communicate with your political representatives in favor of good laws and in protest against bad ones.
    - Communicate with the media or sponsors in protest against any immorallity.
    - Serve in your parish on the parish council, or as lector, usher, sacristan, singer, teacher of CCD, youth or RCIA, in a prayer group or Scripture study group, or help with maintenance and repairs.
    - Serve in your community by works of mercy of visiting the sick, the poor and the prisoners, feeding the hungry, comforting the sorrowful and instructing the ignorant.
    - Use whatever talents that God gave you to bring His Good News to our Culture of Death in the New Evangelization!

Bibliography

Connell, Janice. *The Visions of the Children.* New York, New York: St. Martin's Press, 1992, 1997.

Connell, Janice. *Meetings with Mary.* New York, New York: Ballantine Books. 1995.

Connell, Janice. *Queen of the Cosmos.* Orleans, Massachusetts: Paraclete Press. 1990.

de Montfort, St. Louis, *True Devotion to Mary.* Charlotte, North Carolina: TAN Books and Publishers Inc. 2007

Kraljevic, Svetozar, O.F.M. *The Apparitions of Our Lady at Medjugorje.* Medjugorje, Bosnia–Herzegovina: Information Center "Mir" Medjugorje. 2005.

Fanzaga, Padre Livio. *La Madonna Prepara per il Mondo un futuro di Pace.* Italy: Editrica Shalom. 2002.

Laurentin, René. *The Apparitions at Medjugorje Prolonged.* Milford, Ohio: The Riehle Foundation. 1987.

Dan Lynch Productions

Our Lady of America, Our Hope for the States

- The only canonically approved devotion that is based upon apparitions of Our Lady in the United States.
- Our Lady of America's apparitions, messages and requests for Purity and Peace and her promise of Protection.
- The Divine Indwelling of the Most Holy Trinity.

Our Lady of Guadalupe, Hope for the World

"*This **book** will instruct, encourage and inspire a wide variety of people in the Church and outside the Church.*"
Fr. Frank Pavone
National Director of Priests for Life

The Journal contains all of the visions, revelations and messages of Jesus in the Jesus King of All Nations Devotion.

"*One must read the full account of The Journal to have a comprehensive view and insight concerning the rich spiritual treasures of the Devotion, and the vital apostolate outlined there for our times, NOW TIMES! And get the medal!*" Rev. Albert J. Hebert

Saints of the States

"*This book is a wonderful contribution to appreciate the rich spiritual heritage we possess in the lives of so many heroic men and women of America. Dan Lynch traces the historical development, both secular and religious, through the centuries.*"

"*Dan Lynch has produced a very enjoyable, enriching and inspiring book. It challenges us to do in our times what these holy men and women did in their own.*"
Fr. Andrew Apostoli, CFR

Order Form
Dan Lynch Productions

The Ten Secrets of the Blessed Virgin Mary	Book	$12.95	_____
Our Lady of America, Our Hope for the States	Book	$14.95	_____
Saints of the States	Book	$16.95	_____
Our Lady of Guadalupe, Hope for the World	Book	$14.95	_____
Our Lady of Guadalupe, Mother of Hope	VHS	$19.95	_____
Please specify English or Spanish for VHS	DVD	$19.95	_____
Praying with Our Lady of Guadalupe	Book	$14.95	_____
An Hour of Prayer for Purity, Peace and Protection with Our Lady of America	Booklet	$4.95	_____
Our Lady of America on EWTN	DVD	$15.00	_____
The Journal of the Secretary of the Jesus King of All Nations Devotion	Book	$14.95	_____
Preparation for Total Consecration According to St. Louis de Montfort	Book	$5.95	_____
Rosary Package with Prayers for Life	Booklet	$10.00	_____
Our Lady of America Medal	Sterling Silver	$60.00	_____
Jesus King of All Nations Medal	Sterling Silver	$65.00	_____

Please call our office for other varieties and sizes of medals

Brown Scapular embroidered with an image of Our Lady of Guadalupe $8.00   _____

SHIPPING & HANDLING

UNITED STATES
Value of Order   S & H
$ 0.00 - $ 9.99 $6.00
$ 10.00 - $24.99 $7.00
$ 25.00 - $49.99 $8.00
$ 50.00 - $99.99 $9.00
$100.00 & up   10% of order

-CANADIAN- Double Rates on left

-FOREIGN- Triple Rates on left

Subtotal $_____
Shipping & Handling
(Must be included with all orders) $_____
Optional Donation $_____
Total Due $_____

Method of Payment to John Paul Press

Check Enclosed   Money Order   VISA   MasterCard   Discover

_____   _____
Credit Card Account Number   Expiration Date (MM/YY)

Name as it appears on card:_____

Name:_____

Address:_____

City / State / Zip_____

Daytime Phone(___)_____E-mail_____

John Paul Press • 144 Sheldon Road • St. Albans, VT 05478
Phone 888-834-6261 or 802-524-5350 Fax 802-524-5673
E-Mail - JKMI@JKMI.com Website - www.JKMI.com

Made in the USA
Middletown, DE
19 September 2016